I0822991

Praise for *The Simple Guide to ADHD Regulation*

Finally, a book that gets to the heart of ADHD instead of just offering Band-Aid solutions. Jenna shows us that when we learn to slow down and stay regulated, we're not managing symptoms—we're creating the conditions for our brains to thrive.

—Kristen Bell

Jenna Free offers one of the most compassionate and practical frameworks for ADHD regulation I've ever seen. Her approach is grounded, accessible, and transformative—focusing on nervous system regulation in a way that makes sense for ADHD brains. If you've ever felt stuck in chaos, this book is the guide you've been waiting for.

—Kristen Carder, host of the I Have ADHD *podcast and founder of FOCUSED*

Jenna's strategies go beyond Band-Aids to tackle the core struggles that define the ADHD experience. If you're tired of surface-level solutions that don't stick, this book provides the fundamental shifts that actually work.

—Kelly Baumgartner, ADHD coach and content creator @Kellybaums

THE SIMPLE GUIDE TO

ADHD Regulation

The Secret to Finding Balance, Getting Things Done, and Enjoying Your Life

Jenna Free, CCC

The Simple Guide to ADHD Regulation

Published by Harper Celebrate, an imprint of HarperCollins Focus LLC.

Illustrated by Bethan Richards
Cover design by Gabriella Wikidal
Interior design by Lauren Clulow

ISBN 978-1-4002-5469-9 (HC)
ISBN 978-1-4002-5472-9 (audiobook)
ISBN 978-1-4002-5470-5 (epub)

Printed in the United States of America

26 27 28 29 30 VER 5 4 3 2

CONTENTS

THOUGHT REGULATION FOR ADHD: HOW OUR THOUGHTS AND BELIEFS AFFECT DYSREGULATION

BEHAVIOR REGULATION FOR ADHD: USING REGULATION TO REDUCE COMMON ADHD SYMPTOMS

A NOTE BEFORE YOU BEGIN

You might be picking up this book feeling a sense of urgency, like something is wrong with you and you need to fix it fast. That's how many of us approach "self-help": from a place of pressure, hoping for a quick solution. But regulation work can't occur in a rush. This approach to living with ADHD isn't about quick fixes. It's about slowing down, tuning into yourself, and creating real, lasting change. To move out of survival mode, we have to approach ourselves with patience, not pressure.

I recommend reading this book one chapter at a time and then sitting with the ideas from that chapter. Implement the small shifts discussed before going to the next chapter. This isn't a race; it's a regulation journey. You may be tempted to speed through, looking for the "solution" to your ADHD symptoms, but real change comes when you slow down and let each piece of the process settle into your life. Give yourself space to absorb. Reread. Reflect. Try out some of these changes in your life. The goal isn't to finish the book—it's to live it.

THERE IS NO RUSH.

TAKE A DEEP BREATH.

YOU

ARE

SAFE.

Introduction

KEEPING YOUR HEAD ABOVE WATER

In college, I once asked my roommate, "Do you ever not want to take off your socks at night because then you have to put them back on in the morning?"

Putting on socks was overwhelming.

Everything was overwhelming.

Yet also, just one day earlier, I had written and submitted a ten-page paper right before the deadline, frantically cleaned my dorm room, and was running around campus like a chicken with my head cut off. I didn't understand why sometimes I was *so on* and at other times it felt hard to get dressed. (I've worn flip-flops during Canadian winters too many times to count because of this sock issue.) I was frantic and rushed. Sometimes I felt high, but then I crashed. My energy was so unpredictable that I would *lean into* the extremes. Because what if I didn't have the energy tomorrow? I needed to finish everything now, just in case.

Before I was diagnosed with ADHD, I wondered if I had bipolar disorder. The highs and lows felt so intense and really impacted my quality of life. I have since learned that because of these highs and lows—which aren't often talked about as elements of ADHD—ADHDers are commonly misdiagnosed with bipolar disorder, anxiety, and depression.

After decades of feeling like I was just bad at life, I was finally diagnosed with ADHD at age thirty-two, right in the middle of grad school. At the time, I was also raising two kids under two. The demands of my life had begun to outweigh my coping mechanisms, and for the first time I wasn't able to fake that everything was okay. This was when I started telling my mom that I thought I had ADHD, but she couldn't fathom it. From the outside, I was doing great. I was "successful" in life (if we ignore the four career changes I'd already made by thirty) and had always excelled in school. But I listened to my gut and got an assessment. The results confirmed what I had guessed. Thank the Lord! The ADHD diagnosis was such a relief because it explained so much of why I experienced life the way that I did.

For many of us, an ADHD diagnosis often helps make sense of everything—why we are the way we are, why we struggle the way we do. And that was my experience, too, at least in the beginning. But once I had processed the diagnosis and returned to my everyday life, I thought, *But this still sucks. Life is still hard. I know some of the reasons why, but what do I do about it?*

As I was training to become a therapist specializing in ADHD, I learned that medical and mental health professionals don't really know what to do with us. They'll listen and empathize and provide ideas and tools. I'm sure you've heard it all before: calendars, timers, organizational strategies. But to me these options felt like Band-Aids, with no real solutions in sight. Yes, these coping mechanisms may help keep our heads above water, but is that all we can expect in this life? Just not to drown?

The Predictable Cycle

As I started my ADHD therapy practice, I employed many of the Band-Aid strategies that had been passed down to me, but I quickly noticed that clients returned to the next session not having implemented what we had talked about.

Duh! Whoever thought that giving homework to people who are overwhelmed by the mere thought of putting on socks should be sued!

The good news is that I didn't stay with this approach for long. I started to see that every single person I worked with experienced the same cycle as me: frantically rushing to get it all done (whether physically or mentally or both) and then *crashing*—scrolling on the couch, unable to make dinner (or even decide what to eat).

After hundreds of hours working with ADHDers, it became clear that the ADHD itself isn't our biggest burden. It's that we're stuck in dysregulation, which creates this frantic-crash cycle that makes our symptoms much worse. The bottom line is that we must first deal with this cycle if we want things to improve.

When we look at ADHD through this lens of *dysregulation*, it can be a relief, similar to the clarity of receiving that initial ADHD diagnosis. "Ohhh, I get it! This is why I do what I do!" But the bonus of the dysregulation model is that it gives us answers for how to actually make things better. When I began approaching ADHD management using this perspective, for both my clients and myself, I saw real change. *Transformational* is a word I hear a lot from people doing this work.

The regulation approach I share with my clients in ADHD Regulation Groups—and that I'm sharing with you in these pages—is what allows me to live well with ADHD. This work is the only change I have made in my life, and it has taken me from sockless chaos to present, happy, and productive. I'm providing you with the framework I use in my everyday life—the same framework I see working for my clients session after session. Because I practice what I teach, my life has completely transformed and yours can too.

There is nothing special about my situation. Everyone can experience the benefits of regulation work, including you. Whether you were diagnosed as a child or just recently, you deserve to live a life that doesn't feel so damn hard. You deserve to enjoy your days and not spend all your energy just trying not to drown.

When you get out of dysregulation, you can be more productive, less exhausted, and able to enjoy life with your feet firmly planted on dry land. You've got this!

Section I

Nervous System Regulation for ADHD:

FOUNDATIONAL PRACTICES

Fight, Flight, Freeze, Fawn

THE WAYS DYSREGULATION CAN SHOW UP

ADHD (Attention Deficit Hyperactivity Disorder) is a brain difference that creates symptoms such as working memory struggles, overwhelm, distractibility, and poor time management skills (often called *executive dysfunction*).

Much of the current narrative suggests that if you have ADHD, these symptoms simply come along with it. Because you'll have this brain for the rest of your life, it is what it is. The only thing to do is cope the best you can. Get out those water wings—as long as you don't drown, you're good.

The trouble with our current understanding of ADHD is that the studies done on the ADHD brain don't account for the likelihood that people with ADHD are also dysregulated. This oversight causes us to attribute our symptoms of both dysregulation and ADHD to one thing: the brain we were born with. Our struggles can feel inevitable and, frankly, hopeless. We try so hard to stay afloat, but it can feel like a heck of a lot of work for very little reward.

But once we know that *both* ADHD and dysregulation are contributing to our struggles, there is a lot we can work on to see profound improvement.

When we look at the symptoms of ADHD and the symptoms of dysregulation, many overlap:

- anxiety
- avoiding or procrastinating on tasks
- difficulty concentrating
- dissociating or zoning out
- emotional dysregulation
- extreme sensitivity to sounds, smells, textures, or sights
- feeling fidgety or restless
- irritability
- lashing out
- ADHD paralysis
- people-pleasing
- racing mind
- trouble falling asleep or staying asleep
- sensitivity to criticism

It makes sense that we would place the blame on our ADHD.

But here's what I've noticed: We attribute all of the symptoms we experience to the ADHD brain when in reality, dysregulation is contributing a lot of fuel to the symptom fire.

When we are not aware of the reason for the symptoms, we cannot treat them effectively.

ADHD

Dysregulation

FRANTIC ENERGY

DISORGANIZATION

DISTRACTIBILITY

LACK OF FOCUS

PROCRASTINATION

WAITING MODE

CRASHING OFTEN

FORGETFULNESS

REJECTION SENSITIVITY DYSPHORIA (RSD)

What Does It *Mean* to Be Dysregulated?

Dysregulation means your nervous system is out of balance—too activated, too shut down, or rapidly shifting between the two, often swinging from one extreme to the other. Being dysregulated can get us stuck in fight-or-flight. This is a primal survival mechanism that evolved to help us react quickly to life-threatening situations. But, our biology hasn't caught up with the modern world, where many of us spend our waking hours sitting at a desk or doing school pickups. We're safe at our desk or in our parked car while being stuck in a perpetual state of looking for danger, as if we are still living in the elements, watching out for predators.

This response to mental stressors doesn't mean you think you're in danger. It means your nervous system and subconscious don't know the difference between the psychological stress of a long to-do list and the imminent, life-threatening danger of being chased by a bear. When you are dysregulated, the problem is that most of the time your body thinks these mental stressors *are* life-threatening risks.

One major stipulation I'm assuming as we move forward is that you are typically (hopefully always) in a physically safe space, which I recognize isn't true for everyone. What I mean by "safe" in the context of this book is that for many of us living in the twenty-first century, we're generally not at risk of losing our lives when we're at the laundromat, fixing dinner, or preparing a PowerPoint for work.

But when we're dysregulated, we live as if we are.

In the face of danger (or perceived danger), our systems react in four different ways:

Fight	We confront the threat.
Flight	We escape the threat.
Freeze	We become "paralyzed" or immobile.
Fawn	We appease the threat by accommodating the aggressor.

Note: *When I use the shorthand "fight-or-flight" throughout this book, I'm referring to all four of these reactions.*

When we feel threatened, even if we aren't consciously aware that we're feeling this way, fight can look like . . .

- lashing out at a partner
- being snappy with everyone
- cursing at drivers who cut us off
- irritability
- impatience

When you're in fight mode, your nervous system believes this: "What's happening to me is life-threatening. I need to fight if I'm going to survive. So I'm fired up. I'm fierce; I'm defensive. My survival depends on it."

When we feel threatened, even if we aren't consciously aware that we're feeling this way, flight can look like . . .

- avoiding work until the night before it's due
- avoiding confrontation or uncomfortable conversations, meaning a lot of loose ends out there
- doing easier tasks to convince yourself that you're being productive to avoid the tasks that are dysregulating
- scrolling, spending, substance use, or any activity that allows you to escape discomfort and soothe yourself

When you're in flight mode, your nervous system believes this: "I'm at risk, so I need to avoid this situation at any cost. I'll check out mentally or I'll check out physically. To preserve my own life, I have to get the hell out of here."

When we feel threatened, even if we aren't consciously aware that we're feeling this way, freeze can look like . . .

- needing to pee for thirty minutes, but you're not getting up to use the bathroom
- getting trapped doomscrolling
- being stuck in "paralysis," like a deer in the headlights
- thinking for forty-five minutes about needing to shower instead of getting up and doing it (or deciding not to do it)
- thinking you must pick the exact right thing to do first, so you wind up doing nothing

When you're in freeze mode, your nervous system believes this: "If I engage with this perceived threat, I could die. And so I'm going to lie low. If I don't move, I'll survive. By freezing in this way, this threat won't see me."

When we feel threatened, even if we aren't consciously aware that we're feeling this way, fawn can look like . . .

- never saying no when asked to do something
- preemptively doing all the things that make those around you happy
- thinking you need to do extra to "earn your keep"
- being overly concerned with what other people think
- people-pleasing
- not having fun unless everyone else is

When you're in fawn mode, your nervous system believes this: "I feel inferior, and I don't want people to know and kick me out of the group. Getting kicked out of the group is life-threatening. So I'm going to make myself valuable to everyone. I'll make sure everyone else is happy at any cost, so I can stay safe."

There's a tendency to believe that fawning is more acceptable than fighting or freezing. We think fawning is "just being nice," but is it? Who are we doing it for? I know we're kind, loving people, but we're not fawning to be nice; we're doing it to protect ourselves. There is absolutely no shame in this (there is no room for shame in regulation work). Just be wary of normalizing fawning behaviors because they're actually an indicator that you're dysregulated.

Thank goodness for our ability to kick into fight-or-flight. This alarm system is a helpful one—just not when it's going off all the time. When we're dysregulated, it means we experience one of these four alarm systems—fight, flight, freeze, or fawn—at times when we simply don't need to. We may gravitate to one of these or exhibit all four under different circumstances. When we're stuck in any of these dysregulated states, it makes our ADHD symptoms worse.

Your *Animal* Part

When we're in one of these four dysregulated states, we're operating from what I call our "animal part."

You have your conscious mind, the part of you that chose to pick up this book because you want your life to change. When you're operating from your conscious mind, your prefrontal cortex (responsible for logical thinking, prioritizing, and planning) is firing on all cylinders.

But when you're in fight-or-flight, less blood flows to your prefrontal cortex. You're no longer operating from your logical brain. You're functioning from the survival-focused, primal part of your brain (the amygdala).

I find the work we're about to do most effective when we are more lighthearted. It can help to think of that animal part as a funny little creature, like a chipmunk that takes over whenever you're dysregulated. For example, the place where I can sometimes slide into dysregulation is in the drive-thru line. Frustrated by sitting there for what I deem "too long," my dysregulation can show up. I get impatient and I do impatient stuff, like tense up and yell, "Come on!" in the safety of my car, where no one can hear me. That hyper little chipmunk in me is perceiving my stress as danger and is feeling trapped.

For most of us ADHDers, your animal part shows up in more than just an occasional burst of impatience in the car. When you start to tune in to your dysregulation, you'll begin to see the ways it permeates so much of how you think and act throughout the day. You may *fight* when you're being snappy at your partner. You may *flee* when you're doing every chore imaginable except making that important phone call. You may *freeze* when thinking about your long to-do list and now you're a deer in the phone screen. You may *fawn* when your coworker shares how overwhelmed they are and you've offered to take something off their plate and onto your teetering stack of overflowing dinnerware. You may realize that chipmunk has its sticky little fingers in everything you do and that it shows up everywhere you go.

Why Are ADHDers, Specifically, in Chronic Fight-or-Flight?

Events like a natural disaster or a car accident can trigger the fight-or-flight response, but so can prolonged, less obvious stressors. If you have ADHD, you'll inherently experience more stress because of the world we live in. For example, when you have ADHD, you may . . .

- need to work harder in school than everyone else
- feel like you're falling behind and need to catch up
- feel like you're different
- regularly forget things and have a hard time trusting yourself
- overcommit without being able to follow through, so you feel that you're disappointing people again and again
- feel like you're barely keeping your head above water

These ongoing stressors often experienced by ADHDers can keep us stuck in fight-or-flight. Chronic exposure to cortisol, the stress hormone in the body that is released when we're dysregulated, can put us in a constant state of hypervigilance and overwhelm. This is an exhausting way to live.

Dysregulation doesn't turn off just because it's time to go to bed or because we're on a beach vacation. This can be why we have such a hard time truly resting, such as enjoying the holidays or our favorite TV show, without the nagging shame and guilt playing in the background.

If we want things to get better, the key is to *regulate* the nervous system, the mind, and our actions. Not only is regulation the key to being more productive, less overwhelmed, and more functional in daily life; it also helps you enjoy life and relax too!

"But I Don't *Actually* Think I'm in Danger."

You may find yourself unsure about the premise I've just laid out. It may sound silly that your nervous system thinks it's in harm's way all the time. *You* know you aren't. *I'm in my office writing an email. I know this isn't a life-or-death situation.* And sure, your conscious mind knows that.

But your nervous system doesn't.

This happened to me recently. I went to a virtual-reality arcade with a group of friends. There was a moment in the game where it appeared as if I were walking on a ledge, high

But life is scary and stressful!

When I talk about fight-or-flight only being useful when we're truly in danger, people sometimes respond with something like, "But life really is stressful and overwhelming. There's a lot of pressure on me at work!" Yes, absolutely, but are you in imminent, life-threatening danger? Is there an actual physical threat in the room? No? Then being in fight-or-flight is not going to help you.

up, on the side of a building. When I got to a gap in the ledge, I stopped in my tracks. My brain knew I was safe. I knew I wasn't thirty stories up. But do you think I could make myself step across it? No way. I had to lift my goggles, step forward, and then put them back on to continue. I knew I was safe, but my body and nervous system didn't care—they put me into freeze to keep me alive! Being chronically dysregulated causes a lot of problems (like freezing even when we know we're safe), and we can feel like these problems are our fault. This shame dysregulates us even further. But please know that this survival mechanism is the body and brain trying to keep you alive. It's a biological response that is *not* your fault.

You are not lazy.

You are not incapable.

And these symptoms are not a personal failing.

We just need to reconnect your nervous system, thoughts, and behaviors to your current (and safe) reality so you can relax and function at your best.

I can tell you from personal experience and from working with hundreds of adults with ADHD that getting out of fight-or-flight and into a regulated state is the most impactful way to live well with the brain you have.

I now experience life as a *regulated* ADHDer, and the fact that I am writing this book shows how much my capacity has grown. Not only do I consistently wear socks, but I get dressed every morning, even though I work from home.

Your Permission Slip: You *Can* Say No

I hope you're starting to see the impact regulation can have for those of us with ADHD. However, sometimes our sweet, rebellious brains may view regulation as another "have to" or another "should." Just like with all the tools you've used before, you may feel avoidant because regulation may feel like another rule to follow or another demand on your time and energy. It's important to tackle this work in a way that doesn't feel like a chore, because if there's one thing I know about dysregulated ADHDers, we don't respond well to being told we have to do something.

ADHDers can become avoidant of things we perceive as demands. So rest easy—I will not hold you accountable for how well you cope with ADHD. I hope for everyone to benefit from this work, but I am not the boss—*you are*. I'm not asking you to do what I share in this book. I'm simply offering it as an option you can choose to explore.

The journey ahead is up to you.

What to Expect

Regulation isn't about making you more productive (although that will happen) or more neurotypical to fit in with our capitalistic society's expectations. This approach is ultimately about making life more enjoyable and everything easier. This work is about providing relief.

Ultimately, The ADHD Regulation Method tackles fight-or-flight from multiple angles so we can shake free from this state we're stuck in. We'll first work on regulating our nervous systems and then regulating our beliefs and thought patterns. We will also address strategies to regulate our actions. Over time, regulation can be your new normal.

In the next chapter, we'll start the process of building awareness and taking action to regulate your nervous system—so you don't feel like you're being chased by a bear all day. It's time to stop using so much of your energy just to exist in survival mode.

We do regulation work from the bottom up. We start at the roots (our nervous system) and work our way up to what is visible (our actions and behaviors).
2. Thought and Belief Regulation
Many of the belief systems we hold are a result of us being in fight-or-flight. Without addressing this head-on, our thinking will keep triggering the nervous system back into dysregulation.
1. Nervous System Regulation
Nervous system regulation lets the body know it's safe.

3. Behavior Regulation

Changing the way we do things becomes much easier once we've worked on the first two pieces of regulation. Dysregulation shows itself in the extremes of our actions (all-or-nothing, avoidance, and urgency), and in this phase, we work on finding more balance and sustainability.

The Dysregulation Cycle

THE UPS AND DOWNS OF ADHD

The easiest way to see how fight-or-flight plays out in your own life is in the dysregulation cycle. Whenever I show this to clients with ADHD, they are amazed at how well it reflects their experience.

Living in the *Red*

When we are here, we are in fight-or-flight. It often looks like:

- frantic energy
- trying to get all your tasks done now
- negative self-talk
- overcompensating
- overwhelm
- ADHD paralysis
- perfectionism
- rushing
- urgency

The frantic energy you feel when you're in the red might be external. Maybe you're constantly in a rush and never sit down. It can also present internally, showing up with thoughts like, *I need to take the garbage out, but I also have to answer those emails, and how am I going to get that done before I have to get the kids?* All while lying down or scrolling, in freeze mode.

When you're in fight-or-flight long enough, you will inevitably crash. You cannot be on high alert forever. Nobody can.

Dysregulation Cycle

Rushing

Perfectionism

Overcompensating

Negative Self-Talk

Overwhelm

ADHD Paralysis

Exhaustion

Overstimulation

Exhaustion

Lack of Motivation

Low Dopamine

Understimultion

Living in the *Blue*

When we are here, it often looks like:

- exhaustion
- lack of motivation
- low dopamine
- understimulation

When we've been in fight-or-flight and cannot sustain it anymore, we crash. This is when we dip down into the blue zone. These are the times when you're exhausted and have no motivation to do anything. For some this cycle might be happening multiple times a day, or you might experience a couple weeks of intensity and then you can't get up for days. Round and round we go. The nature of cycles is that we get stuck in them.

One way we can get stuck even deeper in the dysregulation cycle is when we think, *Well, of course I need to get my entire to-do list done today. I don't know if I'll have any energy or motivation tomorrow.* So you push and push. Then tomorrow comes and you've crashed. *See? I knew it. My energy can't be trusted, and I must go hard when I can.* The problem is, this dysregulated intensity is what *created* the crash, but we tend not to make that connection, leaving us stuck on the hamster wheel without any way off.

Words Matter

Recently, a member of my interactive online regulation program ADHD Groups was describing some symptoms of dysregulation and then said, "I hate my ADHD brain." And we all understood what she meant. But I encouraged her, and I'm encouraging you, to use different language. Rather than blaming your "ADHD brain," I'm suggesting that you switch your language to "dysregulation." The reason this is important is because you can really thrive—with the exact brain you have—when you work on regulation. If we think our current struggle is because of a brain difference that will never change, we can become hopeless. What's problematic isn't our brains; it's that our wonderful brains are in fight-or-flight, exacerbating our symptoms. Don't forget that.

The *Alternative* to the Dysregulation Cycle

The whole point of doing this regulation work is for you to build a life that is more sustainable, more productive, more enjoyable, and less exhausting. When we are stuck in the extremes—the red and the blue—we skip right over the middle ground, where we function at our best. You may think you perform best under pressure or in a crisis, but let's look at the big picture. If this were working, you wouldn't be reading this book. Regulation work allows us to live in the middle, where we can access flexibility, choice, and freedom.

Finding *New* Motivation in Regulation

When we are stuck in the dysregulation cycle, the only things getting us moving are fear, urgency, guilt, and shame. It's a big leap to get out of your crash state and into your frantic one, and we need a lot of intensity to fling ourselves back into action. This might make you think you need the bear chasing you to get anything done.

But that's simply not true. As you exit the dysregulation cycle, positive motivators will start to reveal themselves, such as the desire to have something accomplished (by doing the laundry) or feeling good (through exercising). You will take more action and get more done when you're not fueled by fear!

My clients say that once they're more regulated, it's easier to just "do the thing." Instead of thinking about doing something for an hour, they just choose to do it (or not) and move on. This is how things change when fear, shame, guilt, and urgency are no longer your motivating forces.

Now that you've learned about the dysregulation cycle, the next chapters will dive into what to actually *do* so you can work to regulate your mind and body and move toward a more sustainable life.

fight-or-flight

Perfectionism
Overstimulation
ADHD Paralysis
Masking

Negative Self-Talk
Rushing
Overwhelm
Exhaustion

present

clear-headed

regulation

calm and safe

thoughtful and mindful

crash

Exhaustion
Understimulation

Lack of Motivation
Low Dopamine

First Comes Awareness

IDENTIFYING DYSREGULATION

I used to be very confused about my own behavior and the way I experienced life. I'd wake up overwhelmed, thinking about everything I had to do. I'd run through my day in a frantic blur and collapse into bed feeling like I'd failed *again*.

I was constantly overwhelmed but somehow still unproductive. My mind would race with a hundred to-dos, yet I'd sit frozen, unable to start. Every little task felt like a mountain. I was snappy, reactive, constantly rushing, and always behind.

For the longest time, I felt like I lacked willpower, but actually my nervous system was just stuck in fight-or-flight. Over time I've learned: Our behavior is not about motivation or discipline; it's about biology.

Once I understood that, everything started to make sense. And more importantly, I finally knew how to begin addressing my symptoms and let go of the shame that said this was all my fault. You can't shift what you don't see. So this chapter is about helping you *see it*—to recognize dysregulation in your body, so you can stop blaming yourself and start moving toward real, sustainable change.

Here are the first simple steps, starting with:

Action Step 1: Identify Dysregulation

The first step in this work is to become aware of what dysregulation feels like in your body. In the list below, choose one to three signs of nervous system dysregulation that feel most relevant to you. These signs include:

Body Signs

- feeling hot or flushed
- heart racing
- nausea
- physically rushing or feeling rushed internally (which can manifest as impatience or urgency)
- stomach in knots
- tense muscles

Mental Signs

- masking or overcompensation (doing things to hide that you have ADHD)
- negative self-talk
- overwhelm and/or ADHD paralysis
- rumination
- racing thoughts

Begin to look for these signs, which will let you know that you're dysregulated. This skill of in-the-moment awareness is critical. We cannot work on anything we're not aware of.

As you go about your day, notice when the signs you identified pop up for you. Are you rushing to read this chapter so you can move on to the next thing? When you're at your computer writing an email, are your shoulders up to your ears? These are signs of dysregulation.

Curiosity Over Judgment

A curious mindset is helpful in this process. When you're driving and that disagreement with your friend won't stop replaying in your head, you can note, *Oh, I'm dysregulated!* Making it a game where you're *looking* for moments of dysregulation can make doing this work a little easier and less self-critical. Your brain is like a science experiment, and you're here to look closely and observe what's going on. Noticing your patterns of dysregulation can actually be quite exciting!

You may very well be dysregulated all day, every day. That's okay and normal for a lot of ADHDers. The key is learning to see your moments of awareness as a good thing. Noticing dysregulation means you're on your way to major change. Feel free to give yourself a few days to simply observe how dysregulation shows up for you. Don't rush past this step; this is foundational for our work.

Ways We *Soothe* the Discomfort of Dysregulation

Another thing to keep an eye out for are the ways you're soothing your dysregulation. This self-soothing can show up in a number of ways, including:

- bingeing on TV shows, movies, video games, or other forms of entertainment
- nail-biting
- skin-picking
- scrolling on your phone
- shopping and spending
- binge eating
- smoking weed or using other substances

These activities aren't *always* a sign that you're in fight-or-flight, but when they are compulsive, it's likely that you're using them to soothe the discomfort of dysregulation. A sign that something has become compulsive is that you don't want to be doing it, but you don't seem to have a choice. For example, even though you're on a budget, you keep buying things you don't even want. Or while scrolling on your phone, you're thinking, *Put it down*, but you just can't. When we're in survival mode, the body and brain will do whatever they need to do to find short-term comfort.

Q: When I'm scrolling on my phone or if I'm binge eating, it's for the dopamine hit, right?

A: One way to think of these behaviors is, *I like the dopamine rush I get from scrolling on my phone.* But I'd encourage you to reframe it as, *I'm dysregulated, and this thing—the phone, the shopping, the family-size bag of chips—is soothing the discomfort.* These coping mechanisms are a sign that you are dysregulated. As you become more regulated, you'll find that these activities become less compulsive. For now, practice observing these external signs without judgment.

Learning about dysregulation is important and necessary, but unless we implement what we learn, our symptoms won't be reduced. This is a common trap ADHDers can get stuck in: learning and learning and learning and yet not doing anything with the knowledge. So take on identifying your dysregulation as a practice in the next few days before moving forward.

WHAT TO DO:

- [ ] **Write down the one to three signs of dysregulation you selected on page 37. As you go through your day, mentally label these experiences as dysregulation while you're feeling them.**

Once you have the knowledge of what it feels like to be dysregulated and you've practiced identifying it in the moment, you can take action toward interrupting it.

How to Create Change

INTERRUPTING DYSREGULATION WITH REGULATION

I spent all my time in college running. I ran everywhere, not because I liked it or was trying to stay fit, but because I was dysregulated, rushed, and probably late. If I had known then what I know now, I would have walked. That simple change would have been a first step in getting out of fight-or-flight, and my college years could have been a different experience. Maybe socks would have been on my feet instead of flip-flops in the middle of winter.

After we've identified dysregulation, we want to work on interrupting it.

Action Step 2: In-the-Moment Regulation

Once you're aware that you are dysregulated, you now have the choice to interrupt that state. You want to remind your nervous system—again and again—that you are *not* getting chased by a bear. You are safe and can slow down. You are not in imminent danger! I recommend using very simple in-the-moment nervous system regulation practices.

In-the-Moment Nervous System Regulation Practices:

- physically slow down
- relax your shoulders
- take a deep breath
- observe what is in front of you

Here are examples of interrupting dysregulation with a moment of regulation:

- You're writing an email at a frantic pace, trying to get it over with. You notice your impatience, take a deep breath, and continue writing at a more reasonable speed. You may even read aloud as you type. This improves regulation and keeps you in the present moment because you can only say one word at a time.
- You're sitting in traffic with your shoulders up around your ears, willing things to speed up. You notice how tense you are, so you take a breath, relax your shoulders, turn on some music, and connect to the present moment of sitting in the car. You might even start singing in the car—verbalizing is very regulating!
- You're frozen on the couch scrolling, in paralysis. You think, *I really should be mowing the lawn*, but you're stuck. Although you're physically still, you're likely experiencing physical and mental signs of dysregulation that you can practice interrupting, even if you remain on the couch. Relax your muscles, take a deep breath, and come back to the present.

Notice that in these examples, you don't stop driving or leave the email to take a coffee break. Instead, you tell your system that it's safe to keep doing exactly what it's doing. There's no need to change the activity or environment. In fact, I would recommend against it. You don't want the solution to dysregulation to be avoidance; you've done that long enough.

In-the-moment regulation is different from the task-based regulation you may have previously learned. Task-based regulation refers to working out, yoga, meditation, journaling, and other tasks you could check off a to-do list. These approaches are helpful, but relying on them too heavily can inadvertently lead to avoidance as a way to regulate.

If every time you're stressed at work, you leave your office to practice yoga and then return to work and get dysregulated again, you're teaching your system that it cannot be safe or relaxed at work—only at the yoga studio. Instead we're showing your nervous system that (in most cases) no matter how *stressful* work gets, it is still *safe* to be there. Not all stress means actual danger.

Walk *the* Walk

The only way to interrupt nervous system dysregulation is through a physical change—which might look like taking a deep breath, relaxing your tense muscles, or literally slowing down your pace. You cannot talk to your nervous system—it speaks its own language. The only way to communicate that your nervous system is safe is by *acting* like it is, again and again over time. Remember, you wouldn't slow down, take a deep breath, and relax if you were actually getting chased by a bear. So doing so says to your nervous system, "See? No bear!"

Yes, this may sound incredibly simplistic. In fact, you may think it should be more complicated, which is honestly a barrier for some ADHDers. In-the-moment nervous system regulation is sometimes discounted because it sounds too easy—but its simplicity is its magic.

The real power in this work is in the repetition. Just like lifting weights, regulation work requires many reps before we get stronger. But it does not demand perfection. For instance, when you notice you're rushing down the hallway and choose to walk slower, by the time you're at the end of the hall, you may have started to rush again. That's okay. By slowing down, you disrupted the dysregulation. And the next time you choose to slow down, you'll disrupt it again.

At this point, you may be tempted to jump straight to behavior change. *If I'm in paralysis, I need to get up and go do something!* But remember, there's no rush. Behavior change is the last thing to fall into place. It will come, but to get our system out of fight-or-flight, we must start with changing our internal state, not our behavior. As with all regulation work, slow and steady wins the race. So, for now, just work on relaxing your body and being present, even if it doesn't result in "getting out of paralysis" right away.

It's impossible to be aware of every time you're dysregulated, and you won't interrupt it every time you are aware. That's okay. This work is about observing and interrupting fight-or-flight when you can, and you can trust that your awareness and ability to interrupt will improve with repetition.

Action Step 3: External Regulation

In addition to internal regulation, you can also regulate your schedule. This kind of external regulation helps build a lifestyle that minimizes dysregulation from the get-go. While in-the-moment regulation is the core focus of this work, external regulation is the icing on the cake.

Strategies for external regulation include:

- reducing the number of appointments in a day and spreading them across the week instead of trying to get them all over with
- scheduling lunch breaks and rest breaks within the workday
- leaving a night or two open each week to deal with unforeseen tasks such as errands, upkeep of the home, etc.
- scheduling time between engagements to prevent rushing
- limiting yourself to one social event per weekend (if you find you're consistently overbooked and are overwhelmed by it)

Sunday	Monday	Tuesday	Wednesday	Thursday	Friday	Saturday

ADHDers have a tendency to either overschedule or under schedule. We think, *I'll get everything done today so I can have the whole weekend off!* You've probably discovered that this approach isn't very effective.

When I first started seeing clients as a therapist, I thought, *I'll schedule everyone back-to-back in the morning, and then I'll be done with work by 2 p.m. I'll have so much of the day left to do other things!* The reality was that I was so dysregulated by the last appointment that I spent the rest of the afternoon lying in bed. Now I spread my appointments throughout the day, which keeps me more regulated, so I have energy to utilize the time between calls to do other tasks or enjoy a break (instead of just flopping on my bed and doomscrolling until the kids get home).

Break the Cycle of *Busy*

When you're working on regulating, there's an element of trusting the process. For example, if you're working on taking your lunch break and not frantically working through lunch every day, it can be easy to fall into these traps: *I didn't get enough done this morning. I have to work through my lunch hour.* Or, *It's so hectic this week, I'll just work through lunch so I can get it all done, and then I can relax.* The cycle will never end if you do this.

Taking your lunch break may be uncomfortable at first. If you're used to the frantic, fear-fueled energy running the show, it'll feel dysregulating to take a break. But it's important to stick with it! Slowing down will feel uncomfortable at first. Your system thinks the rushing and panic is keeping you alive. On your lunch break, connect with the reality that you are safe and that it's helpful to take time to nourish your body (which is also regulating). Challenge that chipmunk saying "RUN!" We have to exit the cycle somewhere.

Mantras *and* Self-Talk

I want to offer you some mantras that can be very useful in interrupting dysregulation. As we'll unpack throughout the remainder of this book, when we think regulating thoughts, our body is more able to slow down and relax.

Here are three core sayings to help you stay regulated:

1

One thing at a time.

Your brain might be telling you that you must get groceries *and* clean the floor *and* water the lawn now! This is impossible. Remind the chipmunk, “Nope. I can only do one thing at a time, so this is the one thing I'm going to do right now.” Then choose one and begin.

This might feel like I am placing limitations on you, implying you can't handle more because you have ADHD and you have to hold back. That is not the point of this mantra. The point here is that human beings can only ever do one thing at a time. When you connect with that truth and give yourself permission to focus on the task at hand, you will find that you get a lot less overwhelmed and can get a lot more done.

2

Rushing is never helpful.

Believe me, your brain is going to push back against your commitment to slow down. It's going to give you a lot of logical reasons why you need to rush: You're late. Or it's a "crazy" day at work. This is normal. Your nervous system wants to rush, because it's still in a dysregulated state and it's trying to keep you safe. But we know that this is hurting us in the long run, so I urge you to challenge yourself not to fall into these "logical" traps of rushing.

Let's say you're running late to a doctor's appointment. Rushing is still not helpful. When you rush, it *feels* like you'll get there faster, but let's look at the reality . . .

- Best-case scenario? The rushing gets you there 1.5 minutes earlier. Traffic is traffic, whether your stomach is twisted in knots or you're relaxed and listening to your favorite podcast. But when you rush, you arrive so frazzled that you can't focus on what the doctor is saying for the first half of the appointment.
- Worst-case scenario? You're so rushed and dysregulated that you forget your doctor's office moved locations, you head to the wrong address, take a wrong turn on your way to that wrong address, have to make a U-turn, get pulled over, get a ticket, then continue driving to the wrong location. You get there, run into the office—without the paperwork you were supposed to bring—just to realize you're in the wrong place . . . No? Just me? As I said, rushing is *never* helpful.

If you have to rush, there isn't time.

This is for those who like to shove in a few more tasks before leaving the house. If you have to rush to get those few things done, there's no time. Leave it and go. This strategy helps you arrive late less often. We think it's time blindness that causes our lateness, but the culprit is often dysregulation. We feel the need to take advantage of every possible second because "there is always too much to do and not enough time."

This further exacerbates the dysregulation cycle.

Applaud Yourself

I encourage you to celebrate every tiny observation or shift. For example, *Yay! I noticed my dysregulation!* Or, *Wow, I just slowed down for a minute, even though I felt rushed.*

The dysregulated ADHD brain leans toward negative thinking. You've probably noticed that when you *have* achieved something, your brain only feels relief for a moment before becoming overwhelmed again by the next thing on the list. It's what we naturally do when we're in survival mode. If you're in the forest and the bear is chasing you, there's no time to appreciate how far you've come—you've got dangers to assess!

If you don't want to live on the defensive, constantly looking for problems, retrain your brain to focus on the positive changes, no matter how small—even if it's just relaxing your shoulders for a minute while in a meeting. That's a good thing!

If this work feels forced and frustrating, take a deep breath. Regulation is about getting out of the panic and pressure, not "fixing" dysregulation as fast as possible.

Remembering to Do *This* Work

If you're concerned you'll forget all of this as soon as you put down this book, you're not alone. Working memory is a very real concern for ADHDers. Keep it simple. I recommend putting a visual reminder somewhere (e.g., a sticky note on your computer that asks "Regulated?")

Note: *If you already have five hundred sticky notes everywhere, throw them away. They're useless now. Use just one or two—three, max.*

Notice Resistance to the Work

Regulation is most effective if your conscious mind is on board. If you find yourself resisting, let's acknowledge this. It's so important to work through these concerns, because your brain is likely looking for an out. Familiar feels safe, even when familiar is horrible. So if you're skeptical, don't push that feeling aside. Don't ignore it.

When I've invited my clients to share their resistance, they've said things like:

"But I only ever get things done when I'm dysregulated and frantic!"

"This seems too basic."

"Yeah, I know this concept, and it didn't work."

If you were to share these same concerns with me, here's what I'd say:

"I only ever get things done when I'm dysregulated and frantic."

I know you feel motivated only in the frantic state right now, but that's because you're dysregulated. This is what keeps you trapped in the frantic-crash cycle. When we're regulated, we have access to other positive motivators that can help us accomplish more than we've ever experienced before. This work does take a leap of faith, a belief there's something different out there for you. Also, rest assured that this frantic, overwhelmed state will be waiting for you after this work, if you really want it back.

"This seems too basic."

This work is simple when you take it one step at a time, and thank goodness. Can you imagine if I shared ten chapters with a bunch of complicated systems and changes and then I said, "Go!"? You would put this book down and wouldn't implement a single thing. This approach *only* works because it's basic, and that's why I recommend that you pause at the end of this chapter until you've practiced this step for a bit. Slow and steady is the only way to regulate.

"Yeah, I know this concept, and it didn't work."

Knowing about regulation and implementing it are two very different things. Unless you've actively identified and interrupted dysregulation on a daily basis for an extended amount of time, worked through the thoughts and beliefs that dysregulate you, developed more flexible thinking, and challenged urgency and avoidance cycles, you have not done *this* work. We have lots to learn and explore. I promise it'll help.

WHAT TO DO:

- ☐ **Notice and name dysregulation.**
- ☐ **Interrupt with a moment of regulation.**
- ☐ **Build time into your schedule to support your regulation efforts.**

Once you've paused and practiced this for a little while, I invite you to explore more ways to observe dysregulation and to practice regulation. In the next chapter I'll share analogies and visuals to help make this more tangible.

Time and Space are Linear

VISUALIZATIONS TO MAKE REGULATION MORE TANGIBLE

Oh my gosh, there is so much to do today! How am I going to get all this work done, and book that appointment for my daughter, and make dinner tonight? WTF!? My boss just added a meeting to my schedule this afternoon! It's too much!

Ever been here? I have.

Linear and Vertical Thinking: *Time*

Have you ever thought about how you perceive the day?

Because regulation work can be quite intangible, analogies and diagrams can often help us make more sense of it. Dysregulated ADHDers tend to perceive the hours in a day stacked up vertically. We imagine everything we need to do piled one task on top of another. As more tasks drop down on our existing tasks, we try to shift and wedge them in like a game of Tetris. We can feel overwhelmed by the day and feel we should accomplish everything at once, preferably *now*.

Experiencing the day vertically is dysregulating, and it makes us feel like we need to rush and get ten things done at once in any given moment. It sends us into a panic. Why? Because it's impossible to achieve. The reality is, 100 percent of the time, the day is linear. An added task must push out another. When we connect to the reality that we can only do one thing at a time and there are only so many hours in the day, it gives us permission to do what we can and let that be enough.

When we're dysregulated, we tend to perceive the day vertically:

In reality, you can only do one thing at a time. The day is linear, and experiencing it that way looks like this:

You're only one human with one brain and one body. No matter how amazing you are—and, for the record, I do believe you're *quite* spectacular—you can't beat reality. You can only be in one place at a time, doing one thing, twenty-four hours a day.

When you accept the day for what it is, you can be more regulated while living it. For example, if your boss adds an hour-long meeting to your calendar, this requires shifting an hour of your work to tomorrow. Realizing this can prevent you from spiraling every time something unexpected comes up or there's a change in plans.

Consider how this version of the day would feel: You're present in this moment, doing one thing at a time. You can only experience this minute, and then the next one will follow. And the next. Tonight the sun will set, and tomorrow you'll wake up to keep walking along the dotted line of linear time. Can you feel the freedom of that shift? How much more regulating that is?

You might be thinking, *But there's so much to do, and it's depressing that I can't rush and get it all over and done with.* That's dysregulation talking. Your inner self doesn't want to simply get everything over with. It wants to live, experience, and truly take in life, one thing at a time. This is what regulation allows us to do.

When we're dysregulated, we can get stuck in the extremes. You have fifty things to do today, but that feels so overwhelming that you end up doing nothing. When you shift to seeing the day linearly, you're more likely to accomplish tasks on the daily, at a sustainable pace.

The Myth of Multitasking

Have you ever been jealous of your friends or colleagues who seem to do it all, all at once? Or maybe, in your own moments of frantic productivity, you pride yourself on your ability to multitask? I'll let you in on a little secret: There is no such thing as multitasking. Multitasking is actually *task switching*. You can't do everything at once. You're simply pivoting back and forth quickly between different tasks. And spoiler: You're not getting more done. You're just revving up your nervous system and running on fear. If you're a notorious "multitasker," embrace a few days where you intentionally do one thing at a time, and notice how you feel.

Part of the reason you may not have been able to access this fairly simple perspective shift before is because you haven't given yourself permission. For so long, you may have been telling yourself that you're behind and need to "catch up," so you've been rushing and feeling that you aren't allowed to slow down, be more mindful, and do one thing at a time. I am here to say, life will work better this way.

Brick Wall *vs.* Brick Path: Tackling Complex Tasks

In addition to the Tetris analogy, I also like the concept of the brick wall and the brick path. This visualization shows another way we might be thinking about tasks that creates overwhelm. For many of us, we imagine the steps of a complex task stacking up like a brick wall.

Imagine you have a big work project you want to start, but you immediately think of all of the emails you'll have to send, the long hours you'll need to put in, the research you'll have to conduct, the writing, the paperwork—it's all too much!

You see each step of the project stacking up in front of you—until the tasks turn into one giant, towering wall. Those of us with ADHD often think about tasks as "now" or "not now." And we tend to perceive all the steps of a task in the "now" category. But as you stare at the brick wall, it's clear that you simply cannot do everything *now*, like you feel you should. This leads to overwhelm and paralysis, nothing gets done, and you probably experience the added pain of guilt or shame.

When we're dysregulated, we tend to see all tasks and time as being right in front of us, stacked up like a wall.

Here's the shift . . .

Observe that you are seeing a brick wall, and then, in your mind, lay it down to become a brick path. We can only do one thing at a time. So what's the first step you'll take on the path? What is the first brick you will step on? (Note: The first brick doesn't need to be the "best," ultimate, most perfect, exact right first brick. It's just . . . a brick.)

When you practice seeing time and tasks this way, truly embracing the reality that you can only do one thing at a time, the weight lifts. Try it! When you give yourself permission to do just one thing at a time, you can be more present and feel more regulated. (And it's also the only way to make progress in anything. You can't do anything ten steps at a time. That's not how steps work.)

Turn the brick wall into a brick path. All of the tasks and time are still there, but now they're laid out one brick at a time.

WHAT'S YOUR FIRST BRICK?

Just Get Walking

One reason ADHDers can struggle with decision-making (e.g., which brick you should deal with first) is because we're stuck in perfectionism, which is a sign of dysregulation. In essence, we think there's a right or wrong answer. We're obsessed with efficiency and doing things "correctly," because it feels unsafe to take action otherwise. Unfortunately, this can prevent us from walking down that path at all. If you're stuck in choosing a first step, remember that your success will come from making decisions, not the decisions you make. Just get walking.

WHAT TO DO:

- ☐ **Be aware that you're visualizing time like the Tetris model or tasks like a brick wall.**
- ☐ **Shift your mental picture to the dotted line or brick path.**
- ☐ **Take a deep breath, and take just one step forward.**

Play with these mental shifts, and practice using them in your daily life before moving forward. In the next section, we'll delve into how our thinking and beliefs can trigger us to revert back to fight-or-flight and how we can address it.

Section
II

Thought Regulation for ADHD:

HOW OUR **THOUGHTS AND BELIEFS** AFFECT DYSREGULATION

Potential vs. Reality

WHEN WE GET STUCK IN OUR HEADS

As Janet entered her apartment one evening after work, she caught a glimpse of the tall stack of dishes in her sink. Dropping her coat and bag on a chair, she flopped onto her couch and turned on the TV. As a rerun of *Friends* played, Janet glanced again at the sink. Soon her thoughts began to spiral.

I have got to do those dishes.

My friends don't seem to have this problem, so why am I like this?

It's been four days since I've been able to see the bottom of the sink. That's disgusting.

I should have taken care of those dishes after each meal.

Maybe I'll wash them in the morning . . .

After an hour of spinning thoughts about how to tackle the dishes—a job that would have taken fifteen minutes to finish—Janet remained on the couch and the dishes remained in the sink.

Potential *and* Reality

We live our lives in two places: potential and reality. Potential is where we spend a lot of time thinking, judging, and planning. Some thinking, planning, and dreaming about the future is lovely. The problem with most of us dysregulated ADHDers is that we struggle with the "some" and the "lovely" parts. We can put a lot of stressful energy into the "potential"—what we should do, what we could do, self-judgment, excessive planning—but in the end we have nothing to show for it.

Our dysregulated brains feel safe in the thinking. We tell ourselves, *If I'm hard enough on myself, I'll get it done. If I spend twenty minutes making a list of all the things I need to do, I'm being productive. If I figure out how to do this thing in the most efficient way, I'll use my time wisely.* All this thinking and planning can occur with *nothing* actually happening. A lot of energy has been exerted, but we haven't accomplished anything.

One ADHDer's Choice to Align with Reality

"I was at a meeting at work, and my anxiety was through the roof. My thoughts were spiraling. The voice in my head said, *I can't believe I haven't even started that presentation. My boss is going to find out that I suck and fire me.* I was going through the laundry list of things I should do after the meeting, and when I noticed I was stuck in potential, I made the decision to tap into reality. So I said to myself, *The reality is that I'm in a meeting.* And I would repeat that whenever I started thinking about the presentation again. It really helped. I was able to absorb what was being said instead of being stuck in my head when I couldn't work on the presentation anyways." *—ADHD Groups client*

Potential ....

Reality ....

The things we *could* do

The things we *should* do

The things we *should* have done

The *what-ifs*

Negative self-talk

Judgment

Planning and thinking instead of *doing*

The things that are currently, physically happening

For example, I can be grocery shopping, standing in the frozen food aisle looking for peas. That is the reality, but when I float up into potential, I think, *Okay, after this I need to go to the post office and then pick up that prescription. These errands are so annoying. I have more important things to do. I should have gotten groceries yesterday when I had more time. Now I have to rush. Why do I always wait until there's no food in the fridge to get groceries? Maybe I can start meal planning better and get my groceries on Saturdays and then meal prep on Sundays. That would be a more efficient way to do things.*

That frozen food aisle just became a very stressful place to be, when the reality is that I'm just looking for peas.

When you're in reality, your boots are on the ground. You see that you're in the grocery store, and you can focus on finding the peas. You're taking action. You're walking down the brick path. You're regulated!

Dysregulation occurs when we're living in the land of potential because there, we're fighting with reality.

For example, you're stressed because you think you should have gotten the mail yesterday, but the reality is you didn't. You're arguing with the reality that the mail hasn't been picked up yet. This creates dysregulation, uses a lot of energy, and doesn't accomplish anything. Or maybe you're judging yourself for not starting that work assignment. The reality is it simply hasn't been started yet. While you're piling shame and blame on yourself, you're not taking any action in the real world. The work still isn't getting done. When we align our thoughts with reality (and skip out on the *shoulds* and *coulds*), we will be more regulated and more productive.

What living in reality looks like:

Let's say that you remember you didn't call the doctor this morning to book an appointment, and you need the appointment to renew your prescription. When you're aligned with reality, you simply dial the number and make the call now. (Gasp! A phone call? In a timely manner?!) You act and accomplish something instead of spending the morning in a shame spiral about not calling earlier.

When less energy is going to the land of potential, you have more energy to take action in reality.

Strategy

When you notice you're drifting off toward the land of potential, try to ground yourself in reality instead. With your mind or your voice, you can simply state:

The reality is ____________. Now what?

I love the addition of the question "Now what?" because it sets your sights on only the next step instead of spiraling in the past or future. Example: *The reality is that I have not started on that presentation. Now what? Now I will open PowerPoint and start with the title page.*

Why Exiting Potential and Entering Reality *Matters*

Potential takes just as much energy as taking action, but you get nothing for it. The goal of this work is for you to get things done and enjoy your life, and living in potential prohibits that.

Whenever I share this idea in my group sessions with ADHDers, someone in the group will usually push back. I've heard: "This is just how my brain is. It runs a mile a minute. I can't just not think about anything and be present all the time. If I could, I would have done that already." Maybe you're experiencing similar resistance.

You would be amazed at what a difference awareness makes. When you make this work more tangible by separating your experience into the categories of "potential" and "reality," your perspective shifts. The goal is not to become an unfeeling, single-minded robot with no thoughts of the future or past, or of any judgments; it's to prioritize reality over potential a little more than you did before.

Focusing on potential takes just as much energy as taking action, but you get nothing for it.

You will absolutely have moments when you're living in potential, because we're still human beings no matter how regulated we become.

But the more you practice connecting with reality, the

more your nervous system will know that it's safe to let go of the hypervigilance, the judgments, and the overthinking. It will become easier and easier over time to be present with whatever is in front of you without the survival-focused chipmunk standing guard.

Potential Is Not the Compliment We Think It Is

We might think it sounds kind or generous to say someone has potential. We announce it like it's a compliment. But in fact, it can be a nasty word. The definition of *potential* is "having or showing the capacity to become or develop into something in the *future*." That means *not now*. And what do we need to live in reality and be regulated? We need to be here, now!

Potential is like a ghost haunting us: "Ooooh, look what you could be doing if you just applied yourself." "Boo! Why aren't you more successful? You know your teachers always expected you to do great things."

My god, the stress! This catapults us right up into the clouds of shame, shoulds, coulds, and judgments. It sucks our energy, leaving us actionless. So, we don't want to live in this potential space of coulds and shoulds. We want to live in the present. What's real is happening in the now. When we are aligning with the present, we have the power to make change from there.

Three Traps

When we get tangled up in potential, we can get stuck in three traps.

1

***THINKING* ABOUT DOING INSTEAD OF DOING**

The first trap Janet experienced was thinking about doing the dishes instead of actually doing them (or even deciding *not* to do the dishes). It is typical for a dysregulated brain to worry, ruminate, and try to gain control by planning and *thinking* about doing a task. Your brain is trying to protect you; it thinks you're unsafe in the present, and you need to be on alert all the time, thinking and thinking.

Although we can acknowledge that thinking about a task isn't the same as doing the task, our brains can feel that they're being productive simply by being busy. Think of all those lists you make but never use, or the time you spend thinking about how you need to shower instead of actually doing it. Thinking about doing the thing might feel productive, but it's not. At all.

When we spend a ton of time thinking about and planning a task, we often feel worn out by the time we finally get around to doing the task. The time spent thinking and planning can also give ADHDers the dopamine and feel-good feelings that neurotypical people get from actually doing the task. We might feel placated, like we've made progress, when all we've done is make excessive lists. Lists are not the goal. Action is. The only place we get results for our efforts is in the reality of action.

Doing creates results. Being stuck in thinking and judging creates exhaustion.

Note: *You might be thinking,* Duh! ADHD means I have an issue with execution. I know I'm stuck in my head. This is my whole problem. If I could just get up and do it, I would.

When you're regulated, it will be much easier to operate with awareness and get out of your head. And when you learn the strategies we'll discuss in section III, you'll have better tools to help you practice actionable living. Your experience is real and I understand it; I was there myself. But I want to encourage you to consider that this behavior pattern can change.

2

FIGHTING WITH REALITY

The second trap we can get tangled up in is *fighting with reality*. We can spend a lot of time in potential by swirling around in *shoulds*, *have-tos*, and judgment—all of which puts us at odds with reality.

What it looks like to fight with reality:

- I work retail at the mall, but I *should* be doing a job that's more "important."
- I accomplished three tasks on my to-do list, but I *should* have knocked out five.
- I slept until eight o'clock this morning, when I *should* have been up by seven to get to the gym.

This kind of fighting with reality is very dysregulating because it doesn't achieve anything. The reality is you accomplished three things from your list. Feeling shame, guilt, and beating yourself up about not doing *five* things will not change that.

There's no winning when you fight with what is. You will lose that battle every time. This swirling around in potential isn't changing anything; in fact, it's dysregulating you and making it *harder* to create change in the future. Being hard on yourself about not getting "enough" done today will not help you do more tomorrow.

Q: But if I let go of the idea of potential, doesn't that mean my life will never get better? That's depressing!

A: Letting go of the idea of potential doesn't mean your life won't improve. In fact, just the opposite. Choosing to stop dwelling in the land of potential is like letting go of your dream of going to Hogwarts in favor of choosing a school you can actually attend. It doesn't mean your life will never change; it means you're focusing on reality and on what you can achieve in the here and now, instead of letting years go by being lost in your head and not getting any degree at all.

So let's ground our thoughts. Being more aligned with reality is more regulating and might sound like this:

- The reality is I work at the mall. Now what?
- The reality is I got three things done today. Now what?
- I slept until 8 a.m. this morning and missed my workout class. Now what?

From there, you may choose to update your resume, or you may not. You may choose to prioritize those two unfinished tasks today, or you may not. You may put your alarm out of reach so you can't hit snooze tomorrow morning—or you may not. The win of not fighting with reality is ending the internal conflict and using all that energy to accomplish or enjoy something else.

CONTINUED: FIGHTING WITH REALITY

Being aligned with reality doesn't mean we're complacent. It doesn't mean we never make plans. It means we stop fighting a battle we'll always lose. We realize that if fighting with reality worked, it would have worked by now. Instead of hitting our heads against the wall day after day, we live in what's real and take action from there.

As you work on spending more time in reality, be on the lookout for some of the "potential" key words in your thought patterns:

I could . . .

I have to . . .

I regret . . .

I should . . .

I shouldn't . . .

What if . . . ?

These swirling thoughts take us out of the present moment to a place of shame, fear, and dysregulation. And the real kicker is that *none of that is real*!

Q: But the only thing that motivates me is shame and *shoulds*. If I stop fighting an internal battle, I'll lie down and never get up again.

A: Remember when we discussed this earlier? Shame and *shoulds* are just fear. Fear is motivating, for sure, but only in the short term, until you are out of "harm's way." Fear will never get you further than survival. This is why many ADHDers express that when they do achieve something, all they feel is relief, not joy or appreciation.

3

OBSESSING OVER EFFICIENCY

Another way that we can get stuck in the land of potential is when we obsess over "efficiency." Efficiency is a trap for ADHDers. When we're strategizing how to be more efficient, we can get stuck in potential rather than investing that energy into action. Have you been there? Instead of sitting and planning for an hour how to do things in the most efficient way, you could just start the task and be done in forty-five minutes!

Is your focus on efficiency keeping you stuck?

Mental Regulation

Mental regulation can help free you from these traps of potential, and the good news is that you can begin integrating this simple practice into your life today.

Mental regulation is a similar process to nervous system regulation. We identify our mental tendencies to be in fight-or-flight and interrupt them with a moment of mental regulation (or coming back to the present).

Part of the reason I'm so excited about this work is that it's *doable.* You can do this. Not perfectly, but gradually. Simply becoming more aware of those moments when you're caught up in potential is very helpful, because it gives you options. Being able to make the shift out of your coulds and shoulds and back into reality can make such a difference.

WHAT TO DO:

- [ ] **Identify when you're in potential. Notice key words like *should, could, have to, should have,* etc.**
- [ ] **Come back to reality, even for just a moment. (The reality is . . . Now what?)**

Next we'll explore specific thoughts and beliefs that are adding to our dysregulation and learn how to shift these to support our regulated state.

Noticing Your Thoughts

BECOMING AWARE OF BELIEFS THAT DYSREGULATE

I'm behind. I need to catch up. This used to be my constant refrain. In the past, I always felt behind at home, at my job, and at life in general. I was always stressed, even if I was lying down, watching TV, or spending time with friends. This constant, nagging "You're behind!" poking me 24–7 was so dysregulating. Imagine spending your entire life running a race where you're in the back and the rest of the runners are in front. The desperation, the guilt, the shame, the frantic energy! It was enough to paralyze me, having me lying down watching TV more often than not, all the while telling myself, *Get up! There's so much to do! Nothing will be okay until you catch up!* My sweet little dysregulated brain was trying to help me by haunting me with fearful thoughts that I was behind. You'd think this would be a motivator. It wasn't. It just turned me into a deer in headlights and gave me a stomachache.

Our thoughts and beliefs strongly affect our ability to regulate. When we choose to think in a new way, it can revolutionize our lives. I now know I'm always right where I'm meant to be. How do I know? Because that's where I am! How could anything else be true? And my goodness, this truth is not only regulating, but also a very pleasant experience. We're more productive in this mindset too.

When our beliefs and thoughts are more aligned with reality—instead of careening around in potential and fear—our feet are firmly planted on the ground and we can take action. I now spend a lot more time doing things that "catch me up," and when I watch TV, I can truly relax. What a gift!

The Impact Our *Thoughts* Have on Regulation

A dysregulated nervous system forms dysregulated thoughts and beliefs, rooted in fear and urgency. And in turn, dysregulated thoughts trigger nervous system dysregulation. To stop this vicious cycle, we want to work from both sides—our nervous system *and* our thoughts and beliefs.

Consider this thought: *There's not enough time in the day, so I have to rush!*

If we believe this, we will never get out of the dysregulation cycle. Imagine you're cooking dinner. You notice that you're rushing. You want to regulate, so you take a deep breath and come back to the present. But then your brain tells you, *There's not enough time!* Now you're panicking again, distracted by the garbage you meant to take out and feeling the need to pack the kids' lunches for tomorrow. Before you realize it, dinner has burned, you only managed to get the garbage to the front door, and while cutting Johnny's sandwich in quarters just like he likes it, you remember he has hot lunch tomorrow. Beliefs like *There's never enough time* feel true and helpful even, but the reality is they only add to the chaos.

Remember that the brain doesn't care that you're living in the twenty-first century, packing a bear claw into a bento box. It believes you're in the forest, being chased by an actual bear. So the idea that there's not enough time triggers your system to protect itself through fight, flight, freeze, or fawn. None of these are helpful when the tasks you want to achieve require a fully functioning prefrontal cortex. You don't need to rush; you need to prioritize and think logically. If this regulation practice is going to stick, if it's going to be effective, we need to reframe our thinking.

As you work toward regulating your thinking, don't get too caught up on whether your inner dialogue is "true" or not; instead, zero in on whether the belief is regulating. Take my "I'm behind and need to catch up" example. Did you notice that even if it *were* true, the dysregulating belief wasn't getting me any more "caught up"? I was doing even *less* when I held this belief—not more—because it dysregulated me. And a dysregulated me is an ineffective, frozen, and miserable me!

Why Are Some *Beliefs* Dysregulating and Others Regulating?

As mentioned earlier, beliefs are dysregulating when they fight with reality. For example, if I believe I'm behind and need to catch up, I believe *I should be over there*, when in reality, I am where I am. It's a fight that is impossible to win.

When I embrace the idea *I am where I am*, the fight ends and I have capacity to actually do something about the fact that I don't want to be here. I can notice what the reality is and ask myself: *Now what?* I can take a step in the direction I want to go.

Noticing Beliefs That Keep You Stuck

What are some dysregulating thoughts or beliefs that come up for you? Begin by identifying three dysregulating beliefs that you hold. Here are examples of common beliefs from ADHDers that prevent regulation:

Note: If these prompts bring any of your own unhelpful beliefs to mind, jot them down!

- I'm behind. I need to catch up.
- If I rush enough now, I will get caught up and then I can relax.
- Being frantic and overwhelmed must mean I'm being productive.
- This dysregulation is "justified."
- I can't rest until my to-do list is complete.
- There's not enough time in the day.
- Life has too many demands, so I have to rush.
- What I get done is more important than if I'm enjoying my day.
- My regulation depends on other people, my environment, or the amount of tasks on my to-do list.
- I could/should be doing more. It's never enough.
- There's a right or wrong choice to make.
- I have to do things efficiently.

What about you? Are you attached to any of these beliefs?

Get up! There's so much to do! Nothing will be okay until you catch up!

What It Has Looked Like for *Me*

These days, the only time taking care of my home is stressful is when my thinking is not aligned with reality. For example: *I should have cleaned the bathroom yesterday. It's bad that my kids' art supplies are all over the table. I shouldn't be resting when I could be dealing with that pile of papers on the counter.* The reality is the bathroom isn't clean, my kids' art supplies are on the table, and I am currently resting. When I resist that reality, I become dysregulated.

Q: But I really *am* behind and need to catch up!

A: I know that feeling. But has this kind of thinking helped? Has it brought you to a place where you're "caught up?" Do you see how being regulated and in tune with reality is more likely to allow you to do the things you want done?

Remember our question: *Now what?*

The reality is that *I am not done with that assignment yet. Now what?* The reality is that *all my clothes are dirty, and I have not done laundry in a couple weeks. Now what?*

This exercise will be much more productive than being stuck in the potential of: *I should be further along. I should be over there. I shouldn't be here.*

When my thoughts align with reality, I'm more actionable. If the kids' art supplies are all over the table and I want the mess cleared, I toss the supplies on the art shelf in the pantry. If I decide to prioritize something else, the paint and paper remain on the table. That's the reality.

Shifting to Regulated Beliefs to Make Life *More* Enjoyable

Everything we discuss in this book aims to regulate you, offering you a way to enjoy your life and increase your productivity along the way. Isn't that what we're really here on earth for, a better quality of life with fulfillment, enjoyment, and pleasure?

As we choose to release dysregulating beliefs, we can choose beliefs that are more regulating and make daily life more enjoyable. Some of my favorite regulating thoughts include:

- Life is meant to be enjoyed.
- The to-do list will never end, so there's no rush.
- There is the time there is.
- My regulation is important and is a top priority.
- I am where I am.
- I can only do what I can do.
- I can only do one thing at a time.

These thoughts give you permission to take a deep breath and relax and then move forward from there. A big part of you might be resisting. That's okay and expected. We're slowly aligning your system with the fact that you're safe, but there could be a part of you that's still screaming, "But the bear is coming!"

Maybe you're worried that you'll become a blob on the couch and never move again if you let go of the pressure, shame, and frantic energy you generate from the belief that you're behind.

Do you see the themes here? I'm betting this concern has come up each time we talk about letting go of the panic and fear. The chipmunk won't go quietly. It thinks it's keeping watch and saving your life.

Ushering out the chipmunk takes time. The protective little animal probably won't believe you the first time you tell it, "I've got it from here, thanks." This is the work: convincing that chipmunk, through these regulation strategies, that you're okay and it's safe to go.

I want this new way of thinking to be more like *play* and less like work or homework. Play with alternatives to the beliefs that have kept you stuck. Begin to notice which thoughts make you feel better and which ones are more regulating. As you observe your dysregulated beliefs, you can simply say, "I've thought this for a long time. This belief has been running the show. And now I can learn a new set of beliefs that work better."

Have some fun as you identify the beliefs that have been bullying you for too long. Investigate them. Poke them with a stick. Notice how they make you feel and then choose something new.

These new regulated beliefs can be your new mantras. Put them where you can see them and remind yourself of them often.

- Put a sticky note on your bathroom mirror (one, not thirteen!).
- Tape it to your fridge.
- Make it your phone lock screen.

Visual reminders can become invisible after a while, so be sure to move them around from time to time.

Feeling the Tug-of-War

I want to give you the opportunity to notice a few of your beliefs that are preventing regulation right now. Peek back at the list of beliefs on page 97 (or use any of your own), and write down three that you feel are dysregulating you.

Maybe you believe, *I'm behind and I need to catch up*. Explore that! When you try to regulate while maintaining this thought, how do you feel? This is *cognitive dissonance*, where we hold conflicting beliefs, values, or behaviors. It's very uncomfortable and confusing. You've been uncomfortable and confused long enough. Instead, let's align your nervous system, beliefs, and behaviors so you can feel confident and clear, everything headed in one direction—toward ease, productivity, and enjoyment!

If this all feels too forced and you're having a hard time because these practices don't feel true, you might start with what you *want* to believe. For example, although you might not believe it right now, you might *want* to believe that you don't have to be miserable and dysregulated to be productive. You might *want* to believe that life is meant to be enjoyed. Take those new regulated beliefs and make them your mantras!

Warning: *Your brain will naturally return to the old stuff. That's okay. Be gentle with yourself. Simply notice the old story or belief. Then embrace your new mantra and keep moving.*

WHAT TO DO:

- ☐ **Notice your dysregulated beliefs.**
- ☐ **Shift to regulated beliefs that align with reality.**

Remember to put the new mantras where you can see them often as reminders. You learned your current beliefs and accepted them as truth, and you can learn new ones!

Neutral Thinking

A MORE REGULATED WAY TO THINK

Daily life used to be so overwhelming for me. I would see a form for my son's field trip and think, *I don't have time for this! This is so annoying—didn't I just sign forms for school? I have too much to do today! Life is so painful! Why is simple paperwork so overwhelming? It shouldn't be this hard. Why am I like this!?!* I bullied myself with *judgmental* thinking.

Now that I'm more regulated, I can see a field trip form and think, *Next week's field trip form hasn't been filled out. If I want Henry to be able to go, I'll fill it out today.* That's an example of neutral thinking.

When we're regulated, shame diminishes and we see what's actually happening more clearly. If I want something done, I can do it; if I don't want to do it, I don't have to.

Judgmental *Thinking*

Judgmental thinking—thoughts we add on top of reality—is a common pitfall. For some of us, it's so ingrained that we may not even notice that we're doing it.

A lot of ADHDers' stress comes from the judgment that is added on top of tasks, not the actual tasks themselves. We draw inferences about who we are. We call ourselves lazy. We compare ourselves to others, who seem to approach simple tasks with ease. We get stuck in perfectionism and believe we aren't doing anything "good enough."

Exhausting, isn't it? Judgments are a type of "land of potential" thinking that can create so much suffering.

Learning to *Recognize* Judgmental Thinking

As we learn to distinguish between neutral thinking—aka *reality*—and judgmental thinking, we can begin to make new choices. But first, we have to learn to recognize these thoughts.

REALITY: The flower beds have weeds.

JUDGMENT: My yard is always such a disaster. Suzanne's yard is always so impeccable. What is wrong with me that I can't keep up with it? It's never going to be perfect, so why bother even trying?

REALITY: The floor has crumbs on it, and when I walk across it, I get crumbs on my feet. I don't like crumbs on my feet.

JUDGMENT: I can't believe I have crumbs on my floor. They're getting all over my feet. That is so disgusting. Who has crumbs on their floor? I should have swept yesterday, but instead I was watching TV. Why am I so lazy?

The stress of the flower beds and the crumbs, in these examples, are coming from our judgments about them, not the things themselves.

You weed or you don't. You sweep or you don't. Judging yourself as "bad" or "inadequate" creates stress and dysregulation, which will make you unproductive and unhappy. The weight of our judgment causes us to freeze up or avoid the task even longer. You are taxing your brain twice—once when you recall the task, and a second time when you shame yourself for not having done it already.

But when you adopt neutral thinking, you can choose from a place of reason what you want to do about the weeds or the crumbs. You can weigh whether that task deserves your attention today or not. You can choose to live with the outcomes either way. Living in neutral is much less taxing, and you will get more done.

Neutral Thinking Strategy: Letting Go of *Expectations*

Expectations are another version of judgment that keep us stuck in potential.

Many of our problems aren't truly problems until we compare them to our expectations. This is called a *reality gap*. This is why when we have high expectations of a special night out (every New Year's Eve ever), it's often disappointing, but when we have a spontaneous adventure, it feels really fun even if it was nothing special. We aren't comparing our spontaneous evenings to an expectation of how they should be. We're just living in the moment. This is the power of dropping the judgment—more enjoyment, less stress—and you may find that you have fewer problems than you thought you did.

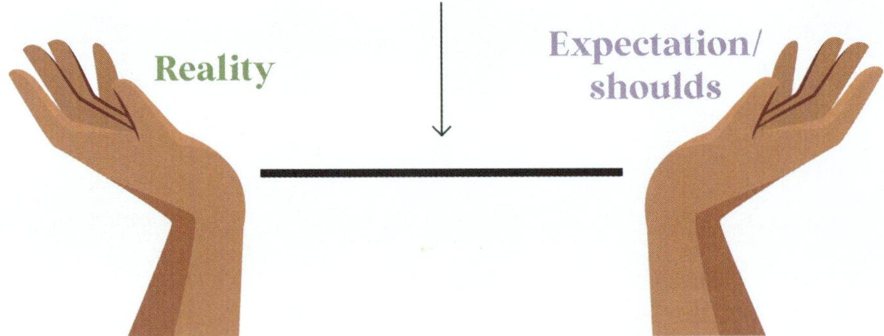

Examples of *Reality* Gaps:

EXPECTATION: My house should always be clean.
REALITY: The kids' LEGOs are on the floor.

EXPECTATION: I should do everything long before it is due.
REALITY: Some things are left until the day before they are due.

EXPECTATION: A forty-five-year-old should be high up the corporate ladder.
REALITY: I just moved to a new field.

When we look at the realities without comparing them to the expectations, are they inherently problems? I would say no.

See how much calmer the reality could be when it is free of expectations? Can you imagine how much less stressful judgment-free living can be? It might be hard at first, but as you replace judgment and expectations with neutral thinking, you'll create new neural pathways that retrain your brain to keep you more regulated.

WHAT TO DO:

- [ ] **Notice where judgmental thinking or expectations are creating stress or problems where there were neither.**
- [ ] **Shift to a more neutral thought and see how it changes things.**

This will be another layer of regulation making it even easier to live in reality, be more productive, and enjoy the journey. Eventually, when a judgmental thought surfaces (it will, you're human), your brain will be better equipped to pivot to the neutral one. This regulation takes time, but your brain can be rewired to think in new ways.

Zooming Out

HOW PERSPECTIVE HELPS US STAY REGULATED

My house has a couple big windows that my boys stand at to look outside. The number of handprints and fingerprints on them is astonishing. Why are their fingers always sticky? And why do they feel the need drag their hands down the window like that?!

Anyway, I used to nag them all the time. "Stop touching the windows. Please don't put your hands on the windows!" No matter what I said, they never stopped. I would get so frustrated! My approach of repeating myself fifteen thousand times didn't seem to be working.

I was sick of feeling dysregulated about something this small, so one day I zoomed out and asked myself: *What is the purpose of this home?* The answer: *To raise my kids and enjoy our loving family.* I realized that clean windows and shiny, tidy appearances weren't actually that important to me. This realization was such a relief—for all of us.

I'm not saying I never get annoyed by the fingerprints, but more often than not, I just enjoy watching the boys as they look outside—no more nagging. I still take my Windex and wipe down the windows now and then, but I don't mind because my kids are enjoying themselves. That's what this house is for.

I bet you have some version of the fingerprints—those tasks and errands and messy moments that gnaw at you and suck all your focus. With the ADHD brain—especially in dysregulation—we tend to zoom *way in*. We get lost in the minutiae. We feel overwhelmed by the small stuff: cooking dinner, washing the car, completing work tasks, wiping fingerprints off windows, etc. Our to-do list consumes our focus. But is this what life is all about? What is all this running around for? What is the point if we're miserable in the process? I refuse to believe that the point of life is to check off to-do lists until we die.

So what *is* the point?

Zooming out is very regulating. We begin to see that what makes us frantic is not what really matters.

Zooming Out

Imagine yourself on your deathbed after you've lived a long life. Ask yourself one question:

"What mattered to me?"

As you reflect on your life, will you glow with pride that you spent a lot of time worrying about what your coworkers thought of you? Will you regret not sending perfect emails? Will you rest in delight that you were always milling about the house, never sitting down to relax? Will you still be worried about the fingerprints on the windows?

When you think about what really mattered, you probably won't be thinking about the small stuff that currently consumes you.

You know that. I do too. So why don't we live like we know this truth?

Because dysregulation is *that* powerful. Our primal brain will override our values, our purpose, and our best intentions when it feels unsafe. This is yet another vital reason to practice regulation—so you can live in alignment with what matters to you!

Countless ADHDers I've worked with have named what's most important to them when they zoom out and look at the big picture. Two consistent themes are:

1. Connection with others (friends, family, partners, children, loved ones)
2. Being present in life and enjoying, or at least experiencing, the journey

Do those resonate with you?

Zooming out gives perspective and allows each small action not to be so heavy and serious. It also allows us to take action and put more energy, focus, and time into what counts.

You may have heard this before, but one way to play with perspective is to imagine that you're ninety years old and you've been invited to come back to relive this one day. How would you spend your time? What would you notice and savor? This helpful mental exercise allows you to zoom out and exit dysregulation for a moment.

You may be resisting this thought exercise because you're telling yourself, *There's so much to get done,* or, *That's a quaint idea, but it's unrealistic*. And I understand. We can't just frolic in fields of daisies all day. But when we're dysregulated, we don't feel like we have *any* time for what truly matters, leading to feelings of emptiness and resentment. We need to loosen the grip. It's safe to, at least sometimes, take a break and spend time with what's important.

The Whole Point:
1. Prioritize meaningful connection to others.
2. Enjoy the journey that is your life.

When looking at your daily life, is enough of your time and energy funneled toward what matters most? Or are you zoomed in on less important things?

Those of us with dysregulated ADHD brains often respond to the realization that we're living out of alignment with our priorities in two ways. We either beat ourselves up for focusing on the small things instead of sitting with our kids and reading a book when they ask. Or we feel so guilty that we soothe ourselves with scrolling, food, or wine. This is particularly true for parents with ADHD—living in rushed dysregulation all day, consumed by the minutiae until the kids go to bed. Once the house quiets down and the guilt sets in, all you can muster is to self-soothe and scroll.

Neither of these responses helps you create the change you want in your life. Judging yourself and escaping to a self-soothing activity are not the solutions to living a life you enjoy. What would the regulated response be?

Zoomed-Out Perspective

Let's look at an example. Say that Jenny's doctor instructed her to avoid stress, as she and her partner were facing fertility challenges. One day, noticing that she felt run-down and needed a break, Jenny considered taking a sick day from work.

Immediately, dysregulation made her feel unsafe, and she reacted with thoughts like:

- *I'm lazy.*
- *My manager will get mad at me.*
- *I really* could *go to work if I'd just get off my ass.*

But as Jenny chose to zoom out, she saw the bigger, truer picture:

- *What matters most to me, in this moment, is growing my family.*
- *Work can wait until tomorrow.*
- *My mental health is worth protecting.*
- *I'm worth caring for.*

By shifting her perspective in real time, Jenny was able to honor what mattered to her, even though the dysregulation was knocking. She lived in alignment with her values and took the day off.

Choosing to prioritize according to your values results in a life that is meaningful, fulfilling, and enjoyable. And yes, you can still balance your daily responsibilities. Beware of your brain lapsing into all-or-nothing thinking with thoughts like: *I'm either taking a day off every time I don't feel like going to work,* or, *I'm never taking a day off under any circumstances.* Regulation is all about the middle ground—the best of both worlds.

Our *Perspective* Is Skewed

Being dysregulated causes us to see reality inaccurately. The little things seem life-threatening, and the big things are pushed aside. Another downside of losing perspective is we are often left feeling numb and dissatisfied with life as a whole—which makes sense! Most of our energy is going to stuff that doesn't really matter. We're constantly overwhelmed and working so hard, but we aren't enjoying our lives. We aren't spending our time connecting with others. All of the hard slog with none of the meaningful rewards.

This can be defeating, but zooming out more often in our day-to-day can help us live in alignment with what matters. Observe when you feel hyper-focused on the minutiae, and see if you are too zoomed in. Take a deep breath and remind yourself what matters. Ask if what you're focused on is in alignment with what you really want. If not, what would it look like to zoom out?

WHAT TO DO:

- ☐ **Become aware of when you are zoomed in.**
- ☐ **Remind yourself of what matters.**
- ☐ **Adjust accordingly and ask yourself: *What choice do I want to make from this more regulated perspective?***

When you bring small shifts like this into your home, your workplace, and your relationships, you may find you are able to spend more time on what matters and less time worrying about the fingerprints on the window.

Section III

Behavior Regulation for ADHD:

USING **REGULATION** TO REDUCE COMMON **ADHD** SYMPTOMS

Flexible Thinking

USING REGULATION TO WORK ON ALL-OR-NOTHING THINKING

In the past, all-or-nothing thinking really threw me into dysregulation when it came to my relationship with food. I used to be either "on" or "off" the wagon. If I'd been eating "perfectly" but then ate a food that didn't fit into this black-and-white way of thinking, I'd think, *Screw it.* Then I'd eat everything in the pantry (and sometimes the gas station chip aisle). This binary way of thinking kept me trapped in a binge-restrict cycle for more than a decade. I believed I needed to be *stricter* with food and that would solve the problem. Of course, it only made the issue worse. Leaning further into extremes of all-or-nothing thinking just pushes us further away from living the regulated, more sustainable life we're seeking.

This all-or-nothing thinking can show up in all areas of our lives and results in all-or-nothing behavior. We're either cleaning the whole house, or we don't bother picking up our clothes off the floor. We're either working on that project until four in the morning, or we're not bothering to even start. We're either exercising five days a week, or we're not moving at all. Not only are these thoughts dysregulating, but they often leave us defaulting to *nothing*. *All* is too much most of the time.

All-or-nothing thinking is flinging us from one extreme to the other. What we're after is "flexible thinking," which is more modulated. It's in the middle.

As usual, awareness is the first step in this work. If you aren't sure where all-or-nothing thinking shows up for you, begin by identifying it in your life. It can be in our relationships:

We're either best friends and talking all the time, or we're not friends at all. At work: We're either going above and beyond and working overtime, or we're disengaged and doing the bare minimum. At home: We're either wiping all the baseboards and vacuuming the couch, or we don't bother hanging up our jackets.

Where do you find yourself getting stuck in all-or-nothing thinking?

	All-or-Nothing Thinking	**Flexible Thinking**
Home Improvement	I either gut this entire room, redo every surface, and buy all new furniture, or I don't bother even painting a wall.	What is one small job I could start with? I'm going to pick a color and paint this room.
Working Out	If I don't have time to run six miles, I won't even put on my sneakers.	I can run one mile before I have to shower for work.
Work Project	If I can't sit down and create this entire presentation, I won't even get started on the outline.	I can work on the outline for a bit before this meeting and return to the rest of the project later.

The Trap

When we are in fight-or-flight, we may believe, *If I only do a little bit, then I'm lowering my standards.* Do you see how that's a trap? Logically, you'll get *exponentially* further if you do *a little bit now* than if you do nothing. This is why we want to practice flexible thinking. And it really is a practice.

What you're doing is retraining the brain to see things in a different way and execute tasks in a different way. And when you start practicing this flexible way of thinking, you begin to collect evidence. You might notice:

- *Oh, now that I've done the outline for this presentation, it feels so much easier to do the next steps.*
- *Oh, when I clean a little bit here and there, it is so much less overwhelming.*
- *Oh, I can get something done even if I don't do all of it.*

When you make new choices, you're collecting evidence that flexible thinking is much more sustainable and productive than rigid, all-or-nothing thinking.

Three Practices

In the following pages, you'll find three simple ways you can practice flexible thinking, but for this week, choose just one to focus on. This choice is a relevant practice, because if you commit to doing all three and take on too much, you'll likely do none of them! So choose only one.

1 Chipping Away

This one's for you if you're that person who won't even start a project if you don't have time to complete the whole thing. Because guess what? If you have to unload the dishwasher, reload the dishwasher, wash the pots in the sink, then dry them, then put away all the dishes, and then wipe the counters in order to take any action at all, that kitchen is going to be a mess for quite a while.

When you make the decision to "chip away" at tasks, you look for one step to take. So maybe you unload the dishwasher, and that's enough. You can make some headway without the overwhelm of thinking you have to complete everything.

Give yourself permission to get really granular with this. I once unloaded just the utensils from the dishwasher and stopped there. I didn't feel like I had time to do the whole thing (which, looking back, was likely inaccurate), but it felt accessible to just do a little piece. I am always looking for a small step of progress I can make toward something I want to achieve—even unloading the dishwasher. After practicing this over time, you'll start to see the evidence that doing little bits feels easier and adds up to a completed task much faster.

Chipping away is an excellent approach for work projects, home tasks, and anything you're avoiding.

2 Consciously Cutting Corners

If you aren't consciously cutting corners, you're most likely unconsciously doing it.

For example, you're working on a presentation, and you have to create a PowerPoint. You've decided that every slide must be gorgeous. You're including a lot of detail on each slide. The problem: It's 9 p.m., you're on the fourth slide, and the twenty-slide presentation is due in the morning. So what you've done—unconsciously!—is cut 80 percent of the content. You did it accidentally, unconsciously, but you did it.

You practice flexibility when you consciously decide it doesn't have to be perfect but done with intention. You're accepting that you cannot put 100 percent into all aspects of every task (it usually isn't necessary either), so you look for what is important and what isn't.

So you're asking:

- What can I cut?
- What is the purpose of this task?

And you put your energy there.

Tip

Ask for help. Maybe what would take you four hours will take someone on your team forty-five minutes. Engaging that team member is a smart way to cut a corner!

If you decide the purpose of this presentation is to let your team know what you learned at the conference you went to, prioritize that and let the other details be less important. So consciously, on purpose, you slack a little on the design aspect. Notice that even when you don't make the conscious decision to cut corners, you already are. And what that looks like is:

- projects being unfinished
- rushing to complete projects at the last minute
- dropping the ball and forgetting important elements

And you likely feel overwhelmed, to boot! So, when you make the decision to consciously cut corners, you're not lowering your standards; you're trimming off edges you don't really need as opposed to dropping the most important pieces.

3 Prioritizing Action

A third practice that helps embrace flexible thinking is prioritizing action.

This one's for the person who gets stuck trying to make things as efficient as possible, or gets trapped in the thinking and planning and can't get things moving. Imagine you need to pull together a report for a client. You may get stuck thinking about the best way to do it. You plan so long about how to do it efficiently, you've now planned for a lot longer than the entire task would have taken you to do. When you notice that you're stuck in the planning, put those hands on the keyboard. It might result in a rough first draft, but when you prioritize action, something is happening. Something is being done.

Taking action that's imperfect is better than thinking perfect thoughts and not finishing anything. (Remember potential versus reality?) Once you've prioritized action, you may have to go back and edit that report for the client, but you've laid the groundwork. Movement has occurred.

So choose one:

1. Chipping Away
2. Consciously Cutting Corners
3. Prioritizing Action

Which one of those three do you think has your name on it this week?

When you begin to experiment in these ways, to make these choices, you are retraining your brain. Rather than getting stuck in all-or-nothing thinking, look for that flexibility in the middle. The more you practice, the more you'll do it without trying. As someone who has now had a very healthy and balanced relationship with food for the past ten years because of this strategy, I can attest to flexible thinking being absolutely possible and completely life-changing.

Note: *You may be thinking,* Duh! I know these tactics. I've tried them. I just can't do them. It's all or nothing for me!

I hear you. When we're dysregulated, approaching tasks with flexible thinking can be extremely difficult. Part of practicing flexible thinking is identifying and disrupting the dysregulated thoughts and beliefs that are preventing you from being able to do part of a task, to do things imperfectly, or to get out of your head and get moving. That is really what we're working on here.

Consistency *vs.* Continuation

Another way all-or-nothing can show up in our lives is in the pressure to remain "consistent" with a certain practice or habit. While consistency sounds like a good thing, it is often another all-or-nothing trap. For example, when you feel that you must do something every day, it can become very dysregulating and fear-based. You develop a rigid way of thinking. You might say:

- *I've got to do it every day, or I won't do it at all.*
- *I've got to do it perfectly, or I won't do it at all.*

We know how this movie ends, don't we? Whether it's packing ourselves a healthy lunch, doing laps in the pool at the YMCA, or working in the garden, I am inviting you to exchange the burden of "consistency" for the gift of "continuation." When you choose a continuation mindset, you're more regulated and more rooted in reality.

A continuation mindset says, "I intended to make myself a healthy lunch every day, but I forgot today." Rather than beating yourself up, saying, "Oh my God! I failed! This sucks! Screw it! I'm throwing in the towel!" you're saying, "Let me get back to that." And the next day, you pack your lunch. It's a much more flexible experience. Our goal is not perfection; it's simply becoming more regulated and understanding the reality that we'll never be perfect. We can always make the choice to return to what we intended to do. This mindset is a lot more realistic. And a lot more will happen as a result!

- You're going to make lunch at home a lot more.
- You're going to go swimming when you can.
- You're going to work on your garden more often.

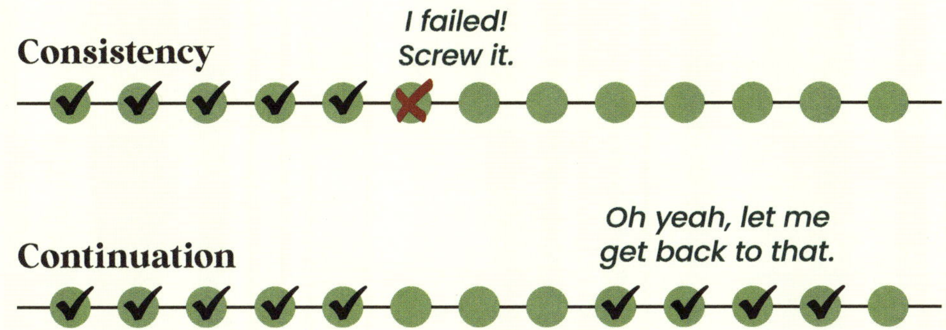

When you decide that the only way to be successful is to make your lunch at home every single day, you're setting yourself up for failure. We're not robots. We're not going to do anything every single day of our lives. Instead, try to make lunch at home the majority of the week, and normalize eating out once or twice on particularly busy days. That's continuation, and this flexibility is going to keep you on your desired path a lot longer.

We can tangibly and actively work on all-or-nothing thinking and shift to flexible thinking. This is one way we can become more regulated. When we think (and therefore act) in a more balanced and flexible way, we will have a much easier time being regulated, reducing symptoms, and improving our quality of life.

A Tool for Your Toolbox

At the beginning of a project, jot down:
What is the purpose of this? Having this through line can help you notice if you're off course. For example, if the point of a project is to communicate brief information, and you've spent an hour choosing a font, you've detoured from the initial purpose. When we get tangled up in the perfection trap, we're in a state of dysregulation. It feels unsafe not to be perfect, but we can train ourselves to notice when we're off course and not aligned with the task's purpose.

WHAT TO DO:

- ☐ **Identify all-or-nothing thinking.**
- ☐ **Practice flexible thinking by chipping away, cutting corners, or prioritizing action.**

Next, we will discuss how this rigid and extreme thinking can affect us. This type of thinking causes us to overcompensate (or mask), which can be an exhausting part of being a dysregulated ADHDer. But we can create more balance!

Masking and Overcompensating

HOW REGULATION ALLOWS US TO ACCOMMODATE INSTEAD OF OVERCOMPENSATE

I had a client who was a receptionist. She explained that the hardest part of her job was "performing" all day. We sat together and looked a little closer. Was that amount of energy really necessary for her role? Or was she masking? *Masking* is when a person with ADHD acts in a "socially acceptable" way to fit in. It might look like fawning—acting particularly bubbly so that people will perceive you as kind and prepared or, conversely, dampening your energy to avoid being seen as "too much."

Masking is a defense mechanism when we feel unsafe. Think of it like wearing a mask, which is a literal barrier between us and others. Many of us have been putting on this show our entire lives, but that doesn't mean we have to keep doing it.

My client worked on reducing her masking for a while and found that she was able to complete her job just as well without all the performance, exaggerated hellos, and intense effort. This helped her preserve her energy so she didn't crash every night after work.

If this sounds like you and you find yourself disproportionally exhausted at the end of a long day or after a night out, I'm with you. This is something I have fallen prey to myself. I can really overdo it energetically in social situations, which makes them tiring. The more regulated I get, the more I see that my high energy levels are not required to have a positive social interaction. I can tone it down and still connect with others and have a good time.

Is It *Safe* to Be Myself?

To reduce your propensity for masking, the first thing to do is become curious about your environment. We have to figure out why you're on the defensive. Try asking yourself:

- *What about myself do I feel unsafe showing here?* Maybe you feel uncomfortable presenting a tired version of yourself out of fear that others will think you're uninterested or rude. (Or you might feel if you show all of yourself, people will think you're weird or too much.)
- *What am I worried about this person thinking?* Maybe you feel if you're not "happy enough," others will think you're disinterested in their friendship.
- *How could I move one step toward authenticity (and in turn, more energy)?* Maybe you want to allow yourself to be sillier and more boisterous! Or maybe you want to feel free to sit back in your chair.

As you dig into these questions, give yourself permission to try out a more authentic version of yourself this week. Explore what happens when you remove the barrier between yourself and the world, and notice how you feel at the end of the day.

As always, it is helpful to bring some nuance to this idea. Some masking is "normal" in our society. Professionalism is a level of masking that almost everyone participates in. I am different with my clients than when I'm out with my friends for dinner. Some of this is pretty typical and doesn't create much harm. But play with dialing back masking where you can to see if you can be less exhausted at the end of the day.

The *Exhaustion* of Overcompensating

Like masking, overcompensation is another example of operating from a place of fear. When we make mistakes, we can experience this gnawing feeling that we're not "good enough." We beat ourselves up and feel that we have to make up for our "weaknesses," which leads to overcompensating: We swing so far the other way that we create more problems than we started with.

For example, let's say you're prone to sending emails with spelling mistakes, and you tend to forget to add attachments, leading to lots of follow-up emails. This can be frustrating and embarrassing, so you meticulously review every email you send. This overcompensation is just as stressful as the mistakes were. You are now so afraid to make a mistake that it takes five times longer to write every email, since you're quadruple-checking the attachment and endlessly tweaking words. Now you have the pain of emails consuming a huge part of your workday, and you're drained. You may even start avoiding emails because they're such an undertaking, leading to a huge pileup of unanswered messages. Overcompensating hasn't really solved your problem; you just have a new, different problem. You're reacting to the fear and swinging too far the other way trying to correct your "mistakes."

I often observe my clients struggling with overcompensation at work—from people working extra hours because they don't think they're getting enough done (even when their boss is saying they're doing good work) to saying yes to every request their coworker has because they feel they need to "earn their keep." When we start becoming aware of this ineffective defense mechanism, we can dial it back and practice living with more balance.

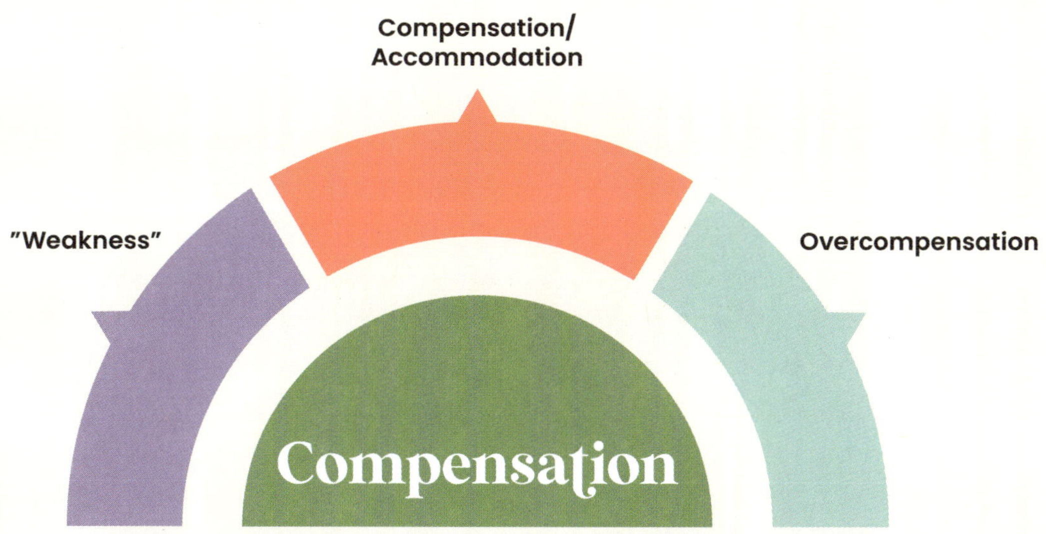

Overcompensation is simply the same amount of pain in the opposite direction.

We are looking to find reguation and balance in *all* areas, including how we cope with "deficits."

Are the tools/behaviors you're using truly supportive of the "problem" or just making you *feel* less afraid?

When we overcompensate, we might . . .

- do extra things at work that aren't in our job descriptions
- do things for people that no one asked us to do
- fill in the gaps for others
- say yes to activities we don't want to do
- do more for a project or task than makes sense

How can we find balance?

- Instead of saying yes right away, get in the practice of saying "I'll get back to you on that." When someone looks us in the face and asks us to do something, we might jump to a yes to get out of the discomfort. Give yourself time to take a deep breath, check your schedule, or maybe even consult your job description. This allows you to be more regulated in what you commit to instead of giving a blanket "yes."
- Which one or two tasks at work cause you the most stress or take the most effort? Check in with how you approach these tasks. Is what you're doing necessary? Where could you preserve your energy and still get the task done well?

Accommodation

Rather than overcompensation, meet its alternative: *accommodation*. To accommodate means to support ourselves—or receive support—in accomplishing tasks effectively. We often think of ADHD accommodation as something granted to us by our boss or school: a quieter working space or more time for assignments. But we can also accommodate for ourselves.

An accommodation can present in a variety of ways, but at its core, it's any tool or strategy you're using that helps you get stuff done effectively and prioritize the life you want to live (hopefully, a regulated one). Unlike overcompensation, which just creates more problems, accommodations actually create *solutions* for your struggles.

An example of an accommodation I use is my (one) calendar. It's a tool that supports my "weakness" of working memory. It's a thoughtful solution that does not take excessive energy or create more stress. It feels like helpful scaffolding supporting me. It's a tool I can stick with without causing more strife in my day.

A calendar tool *could* tip over into overcompensation: for instance, when we feel like we need to write down every little thing or when we spend hours planning the week (rather than taking real action), or when we feel shame if we don't do something that's written down. When it becomes a fear-fueled tool that causes problems in and of itself, that's when you know your accommodation has swung into overcompensation.

What habits or tools do you utilize that might be tipping into overcompensation and creating more dysregulation than actual support? Where can you invite a more regulated response to address your "weaknesses"?

Questions to Determine if Your Accommodation Is Becoming an Overcompensation

- *Is the amount of energy I'm putting into this worth the result? Is my life easier?* If the answer is no, cut it or dial it back.
- *Is this tool solving my problem or creating a new problem?* If you're creating new problems, brainstorm how you can put guardrails on your tool to make it useful to you. Or try a new tool altogether. It's okay to change tactics.

30,000 screenshots in your camera roll of meals you might want to make	an analog recipe card holder, where you've taken time to write down the 10 recipes you actually make
10 lists strewn about the house, collecting grocery lists and random to-dos indiscriminately	1 centralized list on the fridge of all the items you need to buy
23 alarms going off all day, so you've started ignoring them all	3 alarms for the most important stuff: waking up, taking your meds, and leaving for an appointment
35 sticky notes on your desk of all the regulation tips you've been learning	1 sticky note taped to your computer or your car's dashboard
3 different calendars in use (but none of them regularly)	1 calendar or app to log all your events (if it's digital, you don't pressure yourself to use every feature they offer)

Follow-Through Is Not Our Main Problem; Overcommitment Is

When we begin this work, a number of my clients believe that they struggle with follow-through and that they're irresponsible. But usually the problem isn't follow-through; the problem is overcommitting. And it can become a vicious cycle. When we fail to follow through on all the things we eagerly or impulsively committed to, we fear we've disappointed others. So we commit to the next thing to make up for it, and we go around in circles.

WHAT TO DO:

- [ ] **Become aware of when you are overcompensating.**
- [ ] **Find balance by dialing it back. Ask how you can turn your overcompensation into an accommodation.**

Dysregulation shows itself in extremes. We can overdo everything and exhaust ourselves. We can also get stuck doing nothing and exhaust ourselves. We always function best in balance. Next, we'll explore how to utilize regulation to get out of paralysis.

Paralysis

HOW TO PRACTICE REGULATION TO GET OUT OF LIMBO

Maybe you've been here before. You're sitting on your couch watching TV, but your brain is thinking, *I should really take a shower. I can't believe I haven't showered yet, and it's already so late. I'm so lazy. I should be showering right now.* You have to rewind the show five times before you know what's going on. The truth is you aren't watching the show or showering. You're stuck being nowhere. You aren't getting the enjoyment or rest from the show, and you still haven't washed your hair.

This is what I call being in limbo—when our mind is in one place and our body is in another. And it sucks.

We can use regulation techniques to exit this limbo. So let me walk you through it.

1. **Notice that you're in limbo.** In the example above, you notice that your body is on the couch and your mind is in the shower. You're neither here nor there.
2. **Pick a lane.** Remove morality from the equation: There is not a good or bad choice. Getting out of limbo is the win. All you have to do is bring your body and mind back into alignment. The way you exit limbo is by picking a lane. When you "pick a lane," you're either bringing your mind back to your body or bringing your body to your mind.

Here's how this could look. You might have the thought, *I'm in limbo! I'm sitting here on the couch watching TV, and my mind is taking out the garbage. I would like to pick a lane, and I'm tired and don't want to take out the garbage right now, so I'm going to choose to bring my mind back to the show I'm watching. I am giving myself full permission to watch this episode, and nothing needs to happen until it is over.*

You may become present with the show for a few minutes and then think about the garbage again, and that's okay! Be gentle with yourself. We are reminding the brain that it is safe to be present with one thing. The panic about the garbage not being taken out will not get the bin to the curb. If you aren't going to get up and take out the garbage, allow your brain to do the same. Each time we bring the mind and body back together, it's like doing a rep. As you practice, you will build your regulation strength and find that your mind and body stay together more frequently.

If this is a new way of thinking for you, staying on the couch and enjoying the finale of *The Bachelor* may not feel like a big win. But it is! You're training your brain to be present where you are and showing your brain that it is safe to do so. This will contribute to your overall ability to stay regulated.

If you aren't going to get up and take out the garbage, allow your brain to do the same.

Q: But if I choose the TV show, I won't get anything done! How will that work?

A: That is the trick of the ADHD brain: We believe that if we think about something a lot, if we sit in front of the TV for the next hour and don't let ourselves relax, bullying ourselves about how we should be vacuuming, that will somehow get the floors cleaned. It will not. In fact, you'll just be too exhausted and dysregulated to do anything at all. This is another version of the belief: *If I don't have fear and urgency motivating me, I won't do anything.* I hope you're starting to see that this might not be true—that the fear, rumination, and mental exhaustion are actually preventing you from taking action a lot of the time. I find it so much easier to just do the thing when I haven't spent the last hour berating myself for not doing the thing.

If you can live in this way, out of fight-or-flight and present with what is in front of you, you will decide to vacuum more often and you won't be haunted by worrying about it when it's time to rest.

Warning: Don't Negotiate

One caution as you're learning to exit the limbo state by picking a lane: *negotiating*. What that sounds like is, *I'll watch the show, but tomorrow I'm going to do the dishes, mop the floor, mow the lawn, send the invitations, and visit my grandma.* To be clear, that is not the same thing as picking a lane and being present. That's not getting out of limbo; that's making a negotiation with yourself that you're probably not going to be able to meet, creating more dysregulation.

WHAT TO DO:

- ☐ **Be aware of when your mind and body are not in the same place.**
- ☐ **Either bring your mind back to your body, or bring your body where your mind is.**

We've discussed how regulation can help symptoms like all-or-nothing thinking, overcompensating, and paralysis, and now we will dive into how regulation is also at the root of procrastination, distractibility, and impulsivity.

Procrastination

USING REGULATION TO BREAK OUT OF THE AVOIDANCE CYCLE

Procrastinator.

We ADHDers slap this label on ourselves as if it's in the fiber of who we are. We might say, *That's just what I do*, or, *That's just how it is.* The problem with using labels like this is that it prevents us from looking deeper at the root of the issue.

Understanding that procrastination is a typical ADHD trait can feel very reassuring and can make us feel seen, but. . . *then what?* What are we going to do about it? Understanding what's at the root of procrastination is the only way we can work on it. And as we know, dysregulation is often at the root.

Instead of *procrastination*, I prefer to use "the avoidance cycle" because this gives us a richer understanding of what's happening when we procrastinate.

YOU

DON'T HAVE TO BE

STUCK

DOING EVERYTHING AT THE

LAST

MINUTE.

The Avoidance Cycle

Here's what's happening inside:

1. You think of beginning a task.
2. You feel discomfort.
3. You avoid the task that brings discomfort.
4. You feel more comfortable.
5. You solidify the pattern.

You think of beginning a task.
You think about a task you've been dreading—making a phone call to book your ADHD assessment, for example. It's been looming in the back of your mind, but it's so uncomfortable to face, either because you're overwhelmed seeing the whole task at once (brick wall), you're worried you won't do it perfectly (perfectionism), or you feel guilt, shame, and judgment (potential) about avoiding it this long.

You feel discomfort.
You experience the discomfort of dysregulation around the task. Your body is interpreting this as danger, when really, it's a phone call, which is not dangerous at all (I swear).

You avoid the task that brings discomfort.
When you're in chronic fight-or-flight, your body wants to avoid discomfort as much as possible, so it makes sense, for survival's sake, to avoid the uncomfortable task. You may be consciously aware that you're avoiding, or you may not even realize you're avoiding until after you've cleaned the whole house. Meanwhile the phone call still hasn't been made.

You feel more comfortable.
When the task is avoided, your body relaxes a bit. This provides comfort and feels good—for a very, very short amount of time.

You solidify the pattern.
The comfort you experience in avoidance solidifies the pattern of evading the thing that makes you dysregulated. It makes sense to the nervous system, so it becomes even harder to do the task next time.

Of course, you don't want to run away from every single thing that's slightly dysregulating. You want to be able to do whatever you want to do, when you want to do it. But the more you fall into the avoidance cycle, the more solidified the pattern gets. So you may find that simpler tasks are becoming more difficult—because being in this cycle trains your mind and body to avoid uncomfortable tasks until the last second. Or you never return to them at all.

For example, let's say you miss a therapy appointment and feel embarrassed, and to avoid that feeling, you may stop going to the therapist altogether. Or you may choose to cut off a difficult friendship rather than working through the challenges.

Although never on purpose, you're prioritizing short-term relief over long-term success and happiness.

A lot of this work to regulate your mind and body is similar: Awareness + Interrupting = A New Way of Being

You're retraining your brain by interrupting its old patterns and practicing new ones. This is an investment in teaching your system that it is *safe* to do things differently.

The ADHD brain in dysregulation is just worried about surviving right now. It's not worried about your future self. So, survival mode means you're not concerned about your long-term goals. You're only concerned with getting through the day, and avoiding discomfort is a huge part of that.

Procrastination is another sign of dysregulation, which is your body's way of trying to protect you. But I bet these strategies are no longer serving you.

One Reason We Procrastinate: Perfectionism

When we're in perfectionism, we're in dysregulation. When you notice it, I encourage you to ask: "What feels scary? What is the fear?" Whether or not you're conscious of it, perfectionism is a defense mechanism, which shows dysregulation.

Dysregulation says, "I'm in fear. I'm scared. This has to be perfect, or I'll be vulnerable to criticism, which is deadly!"

Regulation says, "It's fine. It's safe for this to be imperfect, and I'd like to do a good job."

Can you feel the difference? There's a line we cross between having healthy pride in our work as a positive motivator and being fearful if our work isn't just right. Remember, perfectionism isn't hurting others; it's hurting you. It's another reason we avoid things, so it's so helpful when we can regulate through it. We're aiming to prioritize our quality of life, and perfectionism will hinder that.

Note: *Part of this work is regulation, being more comfortable, and getting out of chronic fight-or-flight. But another part is growing our ability to be uncomfortable and do the thing anyway. Even when you're more regulated overall, things will still be dysregulating from time to time, and we want to build our ability to feel discomfort and work through it instead of running away.*

Break the Cycle

Next time you find yourself in the avoidance cycle, use these steps to interrupt it and take new action:

1. **Become aware of what you are avoiding and why.**
If you aren't sure why you're avoiding something, sit with it. This may be as simple as sitting down at your computer and looking at your online banking's login page when you're avoiding paying a bill. What comes up for you?

    - Do you feel shame that the bill is late and you know there will be extra fees?
    - Are you confused because you genuinely don't know where to go on the site to pay this bill?
    - Did you forget your login and it's annoying to find it?
    - Are you impatient because you don't have time for this?

2. **Do some regulation work.**
Instead of leaving the task, use your tools: nervous system regulation and thought regulation. Take a deep breath, relax your shoulders, and return to what is in front of you. Observe your thoughts; facing this task instead of avoiding it may bring up some beliefs or worries you didn't realize were there. Use your strategies of connecting with reality and releasing your judgment.

3. **Take a step forward.**

Try logging in to your online banking, and just sit with that for a minute. Logging in might heighten your dysregulation. Observe where you feel this in your body. Remind yourself: *You are safe.*

4. **Notice any progress.**

Perhaps you logged in when you otherwise haven't for a month. Maybe you pay the bill. Either way, notice the progress.

When you start to break the avoidance cycle, it is likely your brain will jump right to shameful thoughts like, *I didn't even get anything accomplished,* or, *I have more bills to pay, and that barely made a dent.*

When you do this, you are punishing your brain for finally doing what you wanted it to do. That won't work. Think of your brain like a child. If you told Johnny to clean his room for a week and he didn't pick up a thing, but then on Saturday he put his clothes in the laundry basket and tidied some toys, would you motivate him by pointing out all the areas he didn't clean? Would you berate him for taking so long? No! You would focus on the behavior you want to see more of and celebrate it!

Do the same thing with your brain. Celebrate when you are headed in the direction you want to go. In this example, if you logged in or even paid the bill? Yay! Congratulate yourself. Speak kindly and recognize how great it is that you did something challenging that you were resisting previously. When you are headed in the right direction, don't discourage yourself from continuing down that path.

Intentionally confronting uncomfortable things creates evidence that working through discomfort is safe to do. When you come out alive on the other side of the task (and maybe even feeling good about the progress you've made), you start to retrain the brain to stop avoiding and start taking small steps.

I would never expect you (or anyone) to do this every single time you're avoiding something. Regulation work is uncomfortable. But if you're sick of your finances haunting you, if you have a weekly task at work that is so daunting and you're ready for that to change, it's time to break the cycle. I promise that the discomfort lessens each time, and soon you may find that you aren't dysregulated about tasks that used to feel impossible.

WHAT TO DO:

- ☐ **Identify when you are in the avoidance cycle.**
- ☐ **Face the task and take one step toward it.**
- ☐ **Congratulate yourself for moving in the direction you want to head. Any step forward is a major win.**

Now let's look at how we can get trapped in the opposite direction: the urgency cycle.

Remind yourself:
You are safe.

Distractibility

USING REGULATION TO BREAK OUT OF THE URGENCY CYCLE

There's a stereotype that ADHDers can't sit still, can't focus on one thing, and are easily distractible, and I know in the past that absolutely has been true for me. When my husband and I were first dating, I remember him coming over and bringing his laptop to do some work. I was watching TV while he was working, and I said, "How can you sit there and work for that long? I could never do that."

It probably hadn't even been an hour.

I'd start working and have a thought like, *Oh no, I forgot to take my vitamins today. I'll quickly go do that*. Then I'd start working again and another thought would pop up. *That table over there is so messy. I'll focus better when it's clean*. And off I'd go. Three hours later I'd have accomplished everything except the work that was due.

This is the urgency cycle—the opposite extreme of the avoidance cycle. It's when you feel you can't *not* do that thing you just thought of. It can be slightly comical, but after decades of not being able to choose what you want to do and just do it, living in the urgency cycle doesn't feel very funny.

The amazing news is that we can work on breaking this cycle too.

When you're in the urgency cycle, you are distractible. You have a thought, and all of a sudden, it's the most important thing! For example, perhaps you're working and you think, *I should really take out the garbage*. It's not a good time to take care of it, but now you feel uncomfortable, so it feels easiest to get the task done and off your mind. Or, while you're relaxing and watching a movie, you may remember you wanted to buy that face wash, so you're online shopping instead of relaxing and watching the movie. Or while in the middle of writing a book, you may remember that you wanted to repot that plant. I'll be right back . . . (just kidding).

The urgency cycle can operate in conjunction with the avoidance cycle. We avoid until *bam!* Now it's urgent and we have to do it this very second. We can also get caught in the urgency cycle as a means to avoid something else that's more dysregulating. We might refer to that as *productive procrastination*.

The urgency cycle is the opposite extreme of the avoidance cycle.

The Urgency Cycle

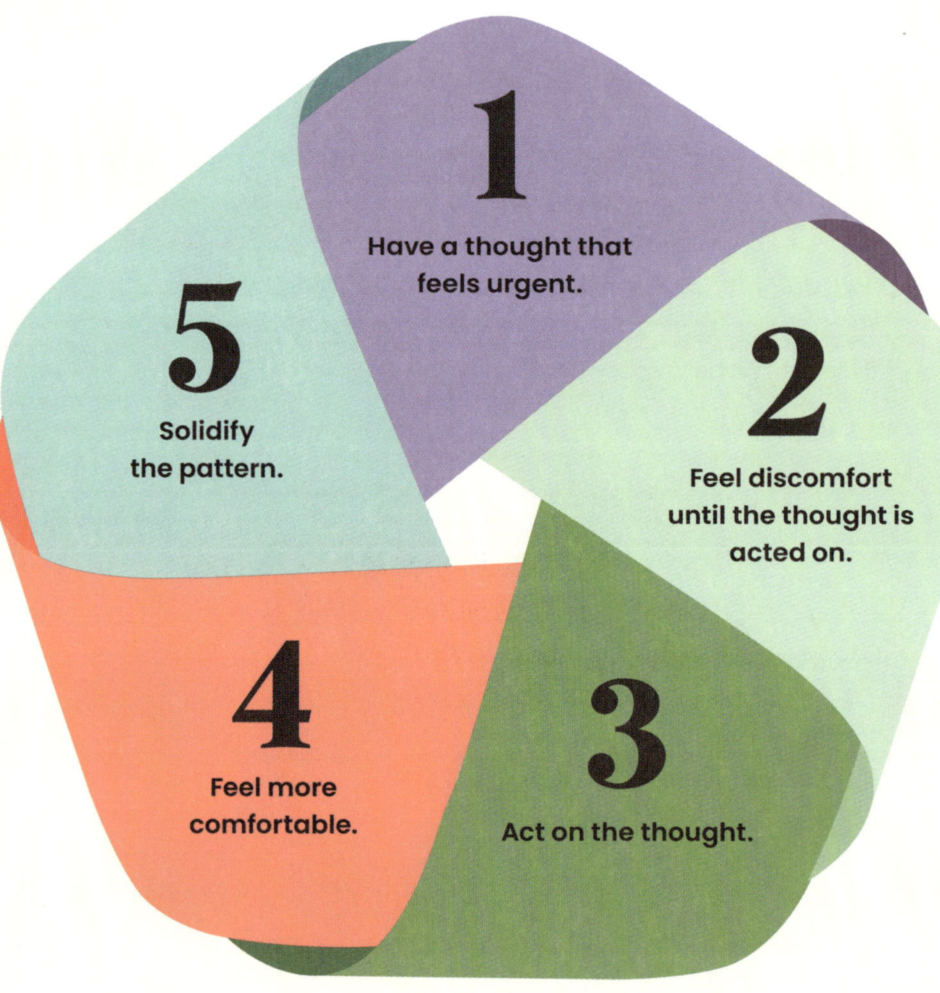

Notice the Urgency Cycle

When we pay attention, we can begin to notice the predictable pattern of the urgency cycle.

Have a thought that feels urgent.
We have a thought that insists that something must be done right now! This may be because we're afraid of forgetting. This is very common, and at the end of this chapter, we'll talk about how to handle this.

Feel discomfort until the thought is acted on.
We can't focus on what is in front of us. We might be squirming in our seats and feeling the sensations of dysregulation.

Act on the thought.
In response to the discomfort, we act on the thought so we can be comfortable again.

Feel more comfortable.
Acting urgently on that (often random) thought makes us feel better in the moment.

Solidify the pattern.
Because we've soothed ourselves by immediate action, we solidify the pattern of jumping up every time we have a thought or an idea.

Breaking the Urgency Cycle

1. **Be aware of false urgency.**
Be aware of the thought and why it feels urgent. One reason might be a fear of forgetting. Or it's a way to avoid what you're currently doing.

2. **Sit with the dysregulation.**
If you want to work on not being someone who *has* to jump up and respond every time you have a thought, then remain where you are and notice the signs of dysregulation. Where do you feel them?

3. **Do some regulation work.**
Remain with the current task, even if it's hard to focus for a bit. Yes, it's normal to think, *If I just go do it quickly, I can come back and focus*, but then you're reinforcing that cycle. Short-term discomfort, and the sacrifice of sitting there unfocused for a bit, is worth it because you'll be better able to stay on task in the future. Some of my clients share that it can be an external trigger, like email notifications, that creates an urgent thought. If you do not want to interrupt your work every time an email comes in, you can practice not jumping right into answering the email, setting a timer for twenty minutes, and checking it then. This is retraining the brain that it is safe to wait and do the task when you choose to.

When you don't engage in the urgency and stay present, your brain will resist. You already know this. It may sound like a little voice that badgers, *Yeah but . . . what if I forget? I must do it now!* I completely understand the fear of forgetting. Working memory can be a challenge for us, even in a regulated state.

The *Fear* of Forgetting

The fear of forgetting is common. Repeatedly forgetting can be frustrating. But no matter how annoying this trait is, we usually overcompensate, creating problems in the other extreme, as we discussed earlier. Living in fear of forgetting isn't doing us any favors.

Here is a creative way to practice flexible thinking when it comes to the fear of forgetting, going from the extremes of overcompensating to a more balanced and helpful accommodation: Put the things you want to remember into three different tiers.

Top-Tier

These tasks will have serious consequences if you forget them. For example, if I have to pick up my kids from school early and forget, the results won't be good. My kids will be scared, the school will call wondering where I am, and I'll certainly have a small panic attack. For this type of thought, I don't mind interrupting what I'm doing and setting an alarm or making sure to write it in my calendar.

Top-Tier Tool: *Acting immediately on top-tier priorities is reasonable! Consciously choosing to do something in a timely manner doesn't mean you're stuck in the urgency cycle; it is only when thoughts become compulsive and universal that the urgency becomes a problem.*

Bottom-Tier

We should be so *lucky* to forget these items! If you never remembered these things, you wouldn't even know you forgot them: a new hair product your friend told you about, a face serum you saw on TikTok, the name of an interesting movie, the age of an actor, the 225 tabs open on your desktop right now, the screenshots in your camera roll, etc.

A client once joined our coaching call and said, "Oh my gosh, my computer shut down and closed my two hundred open tabs." I said, "What a blessing! If you have two hundred tabs open, they are useless." When we hold on to bottom-tier thoughts, we take up mental space. We want to reserve this space for the things that matter.

Bottom-Tier Tool: *We don't want to spend our brain space holding on to these less important things when they can cause overwhelm and stress. Close the tabs, delete the screenshots, clear your Notes app. You're good without all that. It is safe to let go!*

Mid-Tier

These are the things I want to get done at some point, and they're somewhat important, but they're also things I won't forget forever. You have a built-in safety net. For example, most house chores fall into this category. I'll eventually notice the overgrown lawn. If I don't mow it *right now*, nothing major will happen other than having long grass. I'm not going to drop everything to mow the lawn when I'm in the middle of working, but I may stop to write "mow lawn" on my calendar. It can be my priority after work.

Mid-Tier Tool: *Jot a note in your calendar—in an available space—as a reminder to do what needs to get done eventually. Or let the thing go! Practice trusting yourself. (This will get easier the more regulated you become.)*

WHAT TO DO:

- ☐ **Observe when you're in the urgency cycle.**
- ☐ **Challenge the cycle with your regulation tools.**
- ☐ **Practice flexible thinking if your urgency is rooted in the fear of forgetting.**

Next, we will explore how we can inadvertently make our lives harder when we're dysregulated and how to get out of our own way and let things be easier.

Letting It Be Easier

ADDRESSING COMMON SYMPTOMS OF DYSREGULATION

By now you likely understand how dysregulation can make our lives much harder than they need to be, but the good news is we can work on making changes to allow life to be easier. Let's revisit some common dysregulation symptoms that make life harder.

#1 Masking and Overcompensating
If we have a fear of failing, we may be tempted to work extra hard. So we labor over writing an email, triple-checking it for errors, making it more complicated than it needs to be. When we observe these overcompensations, we have the choice to dial back. It doesn't have to be perfect.

#2 Frantic Energy
For a lot of us, moving through the world with frantic energy feels familiar and safe. But is it necessary? As we regulate, we may find we have more ease and calm in our lives. This can feel strange, so we add more to our plates. When we finally get in the flow, we might think, *I should start a new master's degree!* (Guilty.) I'm inviting you to begin observing and asking, "Am I overcomplicating this because life started to feel calmer or easier?"

#3 Negative Self-Talk
When we make a mistake or fail—which we will!—we can be tempted to batter ourselves with negative

self-talk. Our systems believe that if we're hard enough on ourselves, we'll get our butts in gear. That's a defense mechanism. It feels very reminiscent of our childhoods, when adults, parents, or teachers may have used consequences and negative reinforcement to get us to change. Spoiler alert: You do not need to carry these adults in your head anymore; *you* are the adult (I know, I was shocked too). And while I know it feels counterintuitive, you'll receive better results if you're able to let go of the mistake and simply move on. Is there something to learn from this and take forward? There won't always be. Either way, carry on and get back into the flow.

#4 People-Pleasing

We all want to be liked, but at what cost? An example of people-pleasing is taking on work that's not in your job description. Another example could be wandering the store aisles looking for a certain beverage for thirty minutes rather than "inconveniencing" an employee by asking where to find it. Being aware of how *fawn* is dictating your inability to ask for help or hold boundaries allows you to work on it so things can get easier.

Observe which of these areas of dysregulation are making your life harder. Pick just one. Can you work on this through the coming week? Ask yourself, *How can I make this as easy as possible?* Being on the lookout for ease and your desire for it can help you kick-start challenging these dysregulated ways that make life more difficult.

Boundaries

One powerful tool you can use to make life easier is to implement boundaries. When we're dysregulated, we lack boundaries. This is typically rooted in the fawn of our dysregulation menu. When you're in *fawn*, you're people-pleasing in a way that is detrimental to you. Perhaps you say yes to social events that you don't have room for because you don't want anyone to be mad. You agree to do things in meetings that you're kicking yourself for once you get back to your desk. Your partner seems irritated by having to put the kids to bed so you jump up and do it even though it's their night.

Creating ease by implementing healthy boundaries sets you up for success. You can put your own needs first. This isn't selfish; it's healthy. You should always be your first priority ("You can't pour from an empty cup," as the adage goes). But also, you deserve to enjoy life and take care of yourself just for you! You're worth it.

It's important to note that boundaries never require anything of anyone else. The boundary is yours, so the only one who can uphold it is you. For example, when you say, "Don't call me after 5 p.m.," this isn't a boundary because it depends on someone else. Instead, a healthy boundary is simply, "I don't answer work calls after 5 p.m." This only requires something from you: not answering the phone.

What *Boundaries* Look Like Where We Work and Live

As we become more regulated, we can practice setting boundaries more easily. When we're more regulated—which means we feel *safer*—we may discover that we're less desperate for everyone to like us or for everyone to be happy all the time.

Start with small boundaries. Maybe you make the decision to ignore texts and calls when you're spending time with your family on the weekend. It's not anyone else's job to refrain from texting or calling you. It's your job to establish and honor boundaries that help you stay regulated and make your life easier. Try creating one small boundary and see how it goes. If it doesn't "stick," practice continuation by simply returning to your intention again. Remember, all-or-nothing thinking is not going to help you. On the next two pages, you'll find a few ideas to get you started.

Boundaries at Work

We can create boundaries at work to help us stay regulated.

- Plan ramp-up time in your day to have a regulated start. Schedule some time at the beginning of the day that's devoted to yourself so you can organize and prioritize before your meetings begin.
- Plan some wrap-up time. Instead of taking calls or diving into that big project right up until the end of the day, allocate fifteen minutes at the end of the day to complete your tasks.
- Prioritize regulation. Keep regulation top of mind, and then do your work from this state, instead of using frantic energy and dysregulated thoughts to motivate you when there's a lot of work on your plate.
- Establish a firm quitting time.
- Turn off any work-related app notifications after a certain time.
- Remove work email from your phone. (Digital boundaries are important these days.)

Boundaries at Home

We can create boundaries at home to help us stay regulated.

- Establish a clear quitting time (e.g., no chores after 7 p.m.).
- Establish a time when you will begin a bedtime routine (not necessarily when going to sleep, as we ADHDers can really rebel against that).
- Delegate chores to others, naming who is responsible for what.
- Cut corners consciously. This might look like setting a time limit for yourself (e.g., *I'll tidy up for no more than thirty minutes*).
- Commit to at least one night a week to do something for you.

Boundaries can be scary because we can see them as all or nothing. Either you're strong and clear with these boundaries 100 percent of the time, or you have no boundaries at all. Boundaries may need to be built over time.

For example, when I started seeing clients, I didn't have many boundaries for when I saw them or how many I would see in a day. Soon enough that wasn't working for me, and I felt overwhelmed and dysregulated. I could have closed my doors to new clients, fearing that my schedule would become unmanageable; instead, I learned to build boundaries. This took some time. First, I drew the line at five clients a day. Any more than that was a recipe for disaster for me. This didn't mean I *never* had a day with six clients, but I worked toward that goal.

Then I added the layer of boundaries on time of day. It was very dysregulating at first to ask my clients if they could see me during working hours instead of in the evenings. But with two young kids, working evenings wasn't serving any of us well.

So then I started asking clients if we could book before 5 p.m. My thoughts were stuck in the land of potential, ruminating about this for months before I took action. I imagined that everyone would be annoyed or mad or that clients would find a new therapist—so many what-ifs! It turned out that no one had a problem with my request, and I could have been working nine to five the whole time.

You may find this too. A lot of your fears around creating boundaries will likely be unfounded. And some of your fears may come true, but your boundaries are still worth setting. You are safe, even if people are annoyed.

WHAT TO DO:

- [ ] **Observe where dysregulation is a barrier to things being easier.**
- [ ] **Focus on your specific dysregulation "sticking point" for a while. Do you struggle with people-pleasing, negative self-talk, masking, etc.?**
- [ ] **Explore if any boundaries could help make this one sticking point easier for your specific circumstances.**

Boundaries can be a supportive practice for regulation and make our lives easier. But what about when we see boundaries as rules and rebel against them? This is when demand avoidance comes in, and that's what we will be addressing next.

Demand Avoidance

SHIFTING OUR PERSPECTIVE TO AVOID PUSHBACK

During my teenage years, my family had a rotating list of household chores to complete. One time I was headed to grab the vacuum to finally get my chore over with, but on my way to the hallway closet, my mom asked, "Jenna, are you going to vacuum?"

"Well, not now I'm not!"

Do you ever find yourself pushing back against anything that feels like a demand? You're not alone. This is what we call *demand avoidance*. The premise is that when we are dysregulated, we have a tendency to see everything as a demand: housework, emails, feeding your kids, going to that sewing class you signed up for, even going away for the weekend. We can see everything as a burden and rebel.

This phenomenon isn't just limited to demands put on us by others; it also includes the ones we place on ourselves. A common example is setting a personal bedtime in an effort to get more sleep. If you tell yourself you need to be in bed by eleven every night but then stay up even later than you normally do, that's demand avoidance. You're pushing back on the boundary you set for yourself.

Demand avoidance is something we all do to different degrees. This can be frustrating, though, when we rebel against every request, even our own.

Being Demand *Avoidant*

ADHDers can be particularly demand avoidant. Here are some reasons why:

- We're prone to overwhelm, and we feel that every demand on us is too much.
- We want to retain our autonomy and control, so we push back on demands placed upon us. When we feel dysregulated, we feel unsafe. Having control gives us the illusion of safety.

How do we work on this? The answer might surprise you.

A *Radical* Thinking Approach: What Do You Want to Do?

The reality is that we don't have to do *anything*. There is nothing you *have* to do, even though our thinking can make it feel that way. The shoulds and have-tos and what-ifs can be so strong that they feel real, but as we've already learned, the land of potential is not reality. So when you remove the shoulds from the equation, ask: *What do I* want *to do?*

Specifically, what does your regulated self want to do?

Your dysregulated self might truly want to lie in bed all day. You might want to order food no matter the cost and say, "Screw you, world! I *quit*!" But that's the dysregulation talking. If your system felt safe and present, what might you do then?

What do you want to do?

When you're asking yourself this, take a deep breath and allow yourself to get your feet back on the ground.

For example, you're lying in bed. The choice is to get up now and experience a slower, gentler morning or wait until the very last minute and rush out the door. It's crucial to remember that there is no right answer. Either choice is available to you. Neither option is dangerous.

The only difference between these two choices is that you either get to experience the morning in a way that is slower and calmer (which *for me* is more enjoyable and allows my day to be more regulated) or you get to lie down longer (score!) and then experience rushing. Maybe the rushing around causes you to forget some of your stuff, or you don't have time to pack a lunch, meaning you'll need to eat out again, which might result in frustration for the rest of the day.

As a regulated ADHDer, you may still choose to stay in bed longer, but the difference between your regulated state and dysregulated state is that you are fully in control of the choice and are neutrally prepared to accept the outcomes. When you give yourself *full* permission to stay in bed, you own that choice and accept that you won't have much time in the morning to get ready. You may choose to cut some tasks, like showering or making your lunch.

Or, as a regulated ADHDer, you may be quite surprised when a quiet voice says, "But I want to get up." And so you mosey out of bed earlier, you brew coffee at home, and you enjoy it from your favorite mug rather than the travel one.

Again, the goal is not to place demands on yourself or even trick yourself into always doing the thing you think is *more responsible* but instead to practice truly choosing what you want.

I typically choose what serves me best, almost always, when I'm regulated. Sometimes a little extra lying in bed serves me best, but most often, getting up when my alarm goes off is my preferred experience. When I'm regulated, I'm able to make this assessment for myself from day to day. We are nuanced beings, and the same decision isn't always going to be the right one for us. Life ebbs and flows!

Releasing myself from the strict rules day to day has allowed me to slowly create long-term changes in my life, such as not drinking alcohol and typically eating what makes me feel good. I do these things now because I *want* to, not because I *have* to. These changes wouldn't have happened if I was feeling forceful and "shoulding" all over myself about it. In the spirit of flexibility, I will also share that I eat plenty of delicious treats and also drink a lot of coffee and Diet Coke. It's not all or nothing.

You can practice this way of thinking:

1. Notice when you're pushing back against a goal, rule, or intention you set for yourself.
2. Release all shoulds. There is *nothing* you have to do.
3. Take a breath, and give yourself permission to disengage from what's dysregulating you. For example, if going to work is bringing you intense frustration, tell yourself, *Don't go to work today.* Sit with this thought for a minute. Observe what comes up. It may surprise you. You may discover you actually want to go to work so you have money to pay your bills and live your life.
4. Remember that everything is a choice. The power is in your hands.

The thing that trips people up with this mindset is the fact that choices and actions have consequences. You might be thinking, *But if I don't go to work, I'll get fired!* Yes, that could be true. So are you saying you want to go to work so you can keep your job? Wonderful, you discovered what you want!

We cannot separate actions from their effects. When you think about what you want, this means *in reality*. Never going to work while also getting paid is a nice idea but probably not an option.

Note: *This is a thought exercise. Allow for some flexible thinking. I am not saying everything is your choice and your fault; I am saying we can shift our thinking to prevent demand avoidance.*

WHAT TO DO:

- ☐ **Observe where you are pushing back on a perceived demand.**
- ☐ **Release all *shoulds* and *have-tos*.**
- ☐ **Ask yourself, *What do I want?***

Remembering your personal agency from day to day, moment to moment, can help with regulation because it gives you a better chance of living in the flow instead of in resistance to the shoulds and rules we place on ourselves.

A Way Forward

REGULATING FOR LIFE

Phew! Take a deep breath.

I know these pages may have seemed like a lot, but I hope you took my advice and went through the book one chapter at a time, giving yourself time and space to implement these practices one by one. (And if you flew through the book in one sitting, that's okay too.) Even so, since we ADHDers can be a little rigid and perfectionistic in our dysregulated states, your brain might be working really hard trying to figure out how to do this regulation work "right."

Instead of looking for a prescriptive right or wrong, invite this opportunity to view your ADHD in a new way.

A *Reminder* for When This Work Feels Risky

I know that doing this work takes a leap of faith. Regulation may not be something you've experienced before, and it may seem like a dream that is just out of reach. Hopefully you've experienced glimmers of it as you've practiced these strategies, but it can still be scary and unfamiliar when your brain is so used to the frantic-crash cycle.

So, I'm inviting you to put your faith in the process. Try it out. Experiment. See what it feels like. And if you don't like it, guess what? The roller coaster of chaos—those frantic highs and the exhausting lows—will still be there if you want to return to that ride.

If you read this book in a few short sittings, return to chapter 3 and start with nervous system regulation. Spend some time with that practice and then go to the next chapter. This work is not meant to be tackled all at once. It is a toolbox. No one does good work while holding a saw, a hammer, and a screwdriver all at the same time. Focus on one tool at a time, and watch your regulation skills get stronger as you go. As you review and consider the regulation strategies you've learned in this book, release the pressure to do it all now.

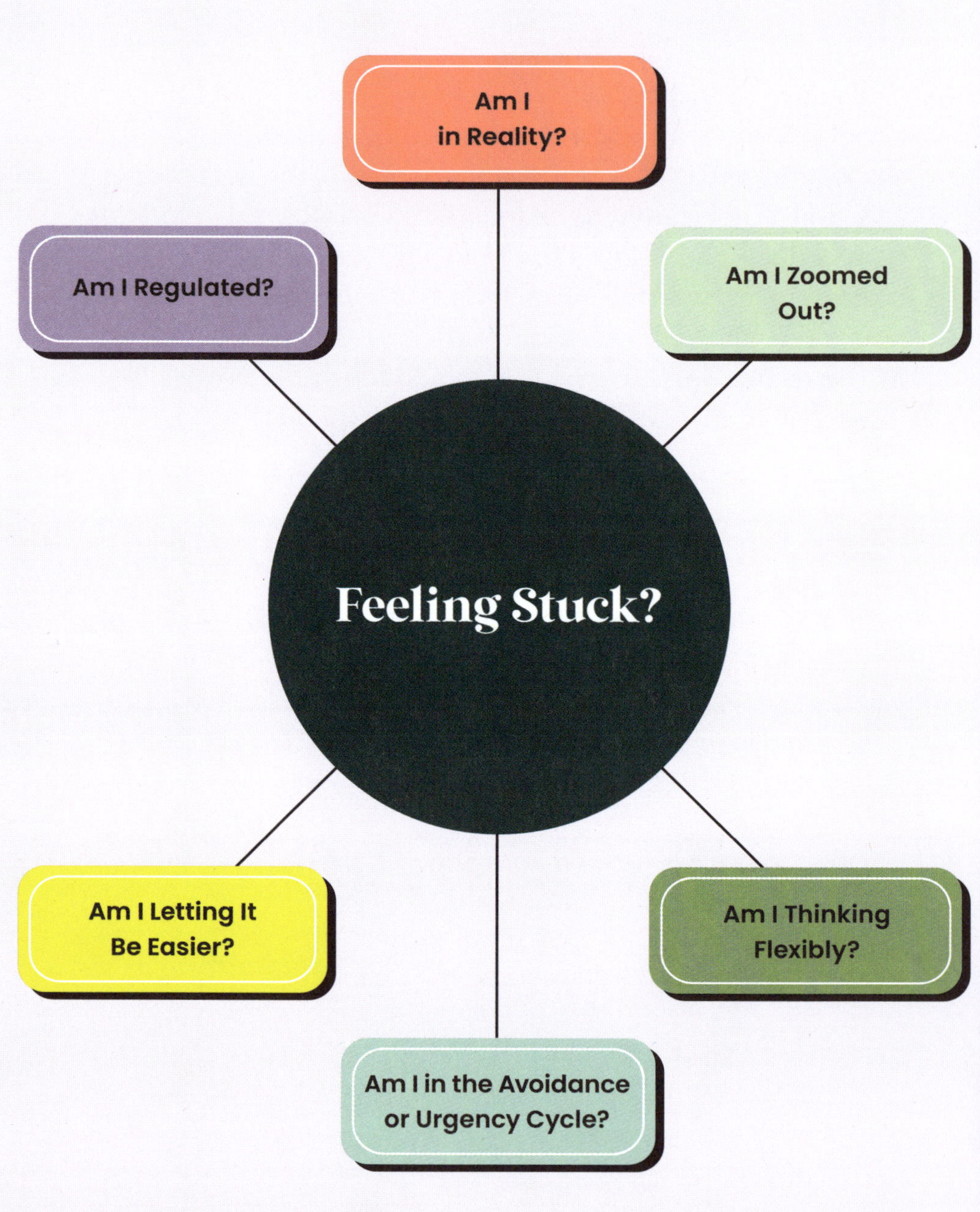
Am I
in Reality?
Am I Regulated?
Am I Zoomed
Out?
Feeling Stuck?
Am I Letting It
Be Easier?
Am I Thinking
Flexibly?
Am I in the Avoidance
or Urgency Cycle?

Here are six questions that can help when you feel like dysregulation is getting the best of you:

Am I Regulated?
Identify dysregulation and observe it neutrally. Interrupt it with a moment of regulation (chapter 3).

Am I in Reality?
Be aware of your thinking and how much time you're spending in the land of potential vs. the real world (chapter 6).

Am I Zoomed Out?
Determine if you're zoomed into the minutiae of the everyday or if you're seeing the bigger picture of what makes a good life (chapter 9).

Am I Thinking Flexibly?
Identify all-or-nothing thinking. When you observe that you're living in the extremes, invite in flexible thinking strategies (chapter 10).

Am I in the Avoidance or Urgency Cycle?
Identify moments when you're procrastinating (chapter 13) or particularly impulsive (chapter 14). What's the next small step you can take to get out of the cycle?

Am I Letting It Be Easier?
Identify where dysregulation is making things harder than they need to be (chapter 15).

A *Cumulative* Practice

And finally, remember that you don't have to apply all these changes at once. Everything above zero accumulates. Every time you choose to interrupt your dysregulation is a success. There's no need to rush. You don't need to be obsessive or intense in this work to see change. The work adds up over time.

If you're stressed about regulation work, take a pause. You can't stress your way into regulation. You can't race your way into regulation. Regulation is not somewhere out there; it's right where you are. Take a breath and remember: You are safe.

I'm excited for you as you continue forward, and I hope that exploring regulation work has opened your eyes to new ideas to consider and that you continue with this work.

You truly deserve a life that is about more than just survival. The cost of having an ADHD brain isn't sacrificing joy and satisfaction just to stay alive. This life can be softer, more enjoyable, *and* more productive. You've got this.

YOU DESERVE JOY.

Acknowledgments

To my clients and the ADHD community: Thank you for taking a leap of faith into a method that asked you to slow down, feel safe, and regulate, even when you weren't really sure what that was supposed to feel like. You believed something new was possible when your nervous system told you otherwise, and that trust has shaped this entire approach.

To my editors and supporters at Harper Celebrate: Thank you, Danielle Peterson, for reaching out to me about writing a book while I sat there with a book proposal, not knowing where to go from there.

To my two boys, ages five and seven: You did not help write this book, but you absolutely helped me practice every regulation skill inside it. Anyone who's lived with two young boys knows exactly what I mean. Thank you for being pure energy, pure joy, and a little wild—often all at once. I love you more than anything.

To my husband: Thank you for being a steady, equal partner, for taking on more at home when I needed it, and for making it easier for me to stay regulated while this work took shape. I couldn't have done this without you.

A final thank-you to my ADHD: It's the reason I could see this work clearly, make these connections, and build something new.

I hope this book helps you see your own ADHD the same way—not as a flaw to fix but as a strength that becomes even more powerful when regulated.

About the Author

Jenna Free is a counselor (CCC) for ADHD *with* ADHD. She specializes in working with the ADHD brain to get it out of fight-or-flight and into working its best, while honoring neurodivergence and all of our uniqueness. She has a focus on making ADHDers lives more enjoyable while also being more productive.

She works with clients through her program ADHD Regulation Groups and teaches other mental health professionals the ADHD Regulation Method in her Certification program. If you're looking to learn more, you can find her on social media @adhdwithjennafree or through her website www.jennafree.com.

Jenna lives in Calgary, Alberta, with her husband and two sons. When she isn't working with ADHDers, you can find her exploring some random new hobby—right now these include acting, tennis, and yoga.